I believe in intuition and inspiration. Imagination is more important than knowledge. For knowledge is limited, whereas imagination embraces the entire world, stimulating progress, giving birth to evolution. It is, strictly speaking, a real factor in scientific research.

—Albert Einstein, 1931

# PROLOGUE

Just like the word *utopia* derives from roots meaning "no place" and suggests a place that does not exist, *uchronia* (alternative or counterfactual history) means history that did not happen, or at least has not been proven real yet by mainstream academia. A neologism originally created by Charles Renouvier in 1876, it originates from the Greek word utopia, replacing *topos* (place) with *chronos* (time), and is typically represented by three types of conjectural work. While one type describes stories of pure fiction taking place in entirely imaginary worlds (like the movie *Pandora*, for instance), another concept of uchronia work is based on established history and represents hypothetical realities. This kind of work, for example, considers what would have happened in history if something else had a chance to happen, like Hitler winning World War 2. The third type of uchronia contemplates the prospect that a particular event did take place during our history, but this noteworthy event went unrecognized or got misunderstood by the intellectual community. This kind of uchronia work sets a path to explore our missed or misinterpreted past. Such an event was the Trojan War, which for centuries we failed to recognize as a real incident until the ancient city of Troy was ultimately found.

So, in contrast, if myths or certain hypothetical events can become real over time, what is really history then? When analyzing the term, history seems to be the formal recognition and ultimately the written account of particular past events that involve human affairs. How do we arrive at our conclusions, though, for past events to become formally accepted? And, is it possible for history to exist without the early speculation that is usually associated with uchronia? The answer is certainly no. If anything, it seems that uchronia works not only help ignite the essential curiosity and conversation that is vital prior to any discovery, but speculations often associated with conjectural history frequently set the ground for history to evolve. Without speculation, "mythical" places like the lost city of Ubar (Iram of the Pillars) in the Arabian Peninsula, or the city of Troy in northwest Turkey, could have never been discovered, and historical events such as the Trojan War could have never been proven real. Time and time again, and more often than we realize, uchronia turns out to be real history.

*"Uchronia? Atlantis Revealed"*, is a provocative narrative that often challenges history and conventional thinking. As a compilation of events from times gone by, it connects several controversial topics and puts forth clues and ideas that could help explain some of the most contentious mysteries of our time. Is the lost civilization of Atlantis real? Is the Old Testament of the Bible a copy of a much older original? What is the meaning behind the Nazca Lines? Is there a secret chamber below the Great Sphinx? These mysteries and others will be explored in vivid detail throughout the pages of this book.

# INTRODUCTION

*Does Humanity Trace Back to a Primary Couple?*
*Real Discoveries of "Mythical" Places*

Why have we not yet been able to expose real evidence that could provide clear answers in the development of human evolution? Why have we not been able to irrefutably establish the origin of the mysterious mutation that "overnight" caused disruptions in human genealogy and triggered the emergence of *Homo sapiens*? Where is the scientific proof to satisfy such important questions? Is it conceivable that the answers reach beyond our grasp, or are they well-hidden beneath layers of ancient texts and religious manuscripts as the church often proclaims?

Today, many theologians insist on the Holy Bible's validity, and further point out that all answers to our hidden past can be found literally inside religious scripts. This, no doubt, is an incredible assertion, but can it be possible? Can religious texts truly help unlock the mystery of our missing past, and should the scientific community continue to study the Bible and other religious scriptures for clues? Certainly, the answer is yes. Indeed, in the last few decades, scientific research has established repeatedly that not only does the Bible contain real history, but even some of its most controversial claims (e.g., humanity traces back to an original couple) are now proven correct after all.

Actually, a recent mitochondrial DNA study conceded that not only does mankind trace back to an original pair or a small group of individuals, but according to the same research, we originated in South Africa approximately 200,000 years ago. Although the study was not specifically clear as to how the "sudden" and "precise" human transformation took place or whether it could have happened naturally, it indicated that humans migrated out of the African continent about 100,000 years later. Of course, such a remarkable scientific announcement not only turned the theory of human evolution on its head but also elevated the possibility of creationism, even among those who never before considered such a hypothesis.

While taking this latest breakthrough into account, along with all past "unbelievable" discoveries that further confirmed other religious claims, why is it so difficult for mainstream scholars to accept the historical significance of religious texts? Certainly, the information our ancestors painstakingly collected, recorded, and safeguarded over the millennia was considered to be of high importance. While time and time again we confirm not only the places cited in religious books but also some of the most incredible details within, why is there such ongoing persistence from the scientific community to often dismiss ancient testimony as groundless tales?

What if, for a moment, we allowed ourselves to take a closer look and viewed the scriptures with a more open mind? Undoubtedly, many stories in the past which were thought to be myths, turned out to be true. In addition to substantiated claims that all humans trace back to an original Adam and Eve, in the last century or so, archaeological discoveries proved that many "imaginary" places recorded in the Bible— as well as in other manuscripts of antiquity—were also real. Not only was it established that such fantastic places were real, but amazingly enough, once they were found, a closer examination revealed that the circumstances and events which surrounded their demise were real too.

For example, the once-mythical city of Troy, which for centuries was thought to be a creation of Homer's imagination, was ultimately found in western Turkey and in the exact geographic location where

Homer had placed it in his story. In the case of Troy, as many established archaeologists refused to search for such a "mythological" place, the burden was taken by Heinrich Schliemann, an amateur archaeologist who ultimately discovered the legendary city by following location tips contained in Homer's epic book, *Iliad*. Could it be then that the rest of Homer's story is true? One thing is certain: after a thorough analysis of the site, which took several decades, archaeologists conceded that the Greeks had burned Troy to the ground, just as Homer asserted in his account.

The infamous cities of Sodom and Gomorrah, which according to the Bible suffered God's ultimate wrath, were also ultimately discovered and are now sites of continuous study. Incredibly enough, and just as the Bible claims, we have also concluded that both cities were destroyed as if by brimstone and fire. Is this just another strange coincidence? While of course elevated traces of radiation among the ruins raise legitimate questions as to what exactly was "brimstone and fire," one fact remains: the once-imaginary cities were real, and the primitive description of their demise, no matter how fantastic it sounded once, turned out to be correct.

So while the scientific community has repeatedly come to agree with many of the religious stories, why is it then that ancient testimony (and most religious claims) are still not given the proper attention? Can this be a classic case of cognitive dissonance? Is it possible that in fear of ridicule, most scientists operate under the automatic assumption that until undeniable proof exists, all ancient testimony must be viewed either as a myth or superstition? Could it be that the dissection of religious scriptures goes beyond the acceptable constraints set by the church? Or perhaps this happens because modern humans are conditioned to adhere only to what they "know" is true. Thus, in our endless pursuit of knowledge, often enough, we don't see the forest for the trees.

# ATLANTIS REVEALED

*Ancient Technologies: Mechanical Computers and Batteries --
Was the Great Flood a Real Event? -- Was America Discovered
by a Bronze-Age Civilization? -- Were Caucasians in North
America in 7000BC? -- Did Bronze-Age Visitors Help "Form"
the Mayan Civilization? -- The Metcalf Stone -- Who Were
the Minoans? -- Atlantis Revealed -- Is the Great Sphinx Older
than the Pyramids? -- The Phaistos Disc: An Ancient Souvenir?*

While, without a doubt, the twentieth century brought to us some of
the most incredible scientific breakthroughs humanity ever witnessed,
we must not discount the amazing achievements and technological
wonders left behind by past human civilizations. Aside from the several megalithic monuments antiquity left behind, there are also many
smaller marvels of ancient ingenuity that confront our awareness and
demonstrate our ancestors' amazing technological abilities.

Recent excavations on the Greek island of Santorini (Thira)
revealed that houses in the 3,600-year-old city of Akrotiri had indoor
plumbing, complete with sewer and water supply lines for both hot

and cold water. This is incredible because up until recently, we were under the impression that it was the Romans who were first able to utilize such technology, nearly 1,500 years later.

What about the Antikythera Mechanism? An extremely complex device designed to calculate astronomical positions at any given moment in time. It was found at the bottom of the Aegean Sea near the Greek island of Antikythera, hence its name. Made out of several bronze wheels and other mechanical components more than 2,000 years ago, this device is so incredible that at first glance, it resembles a twentieth-century piece of equipment. Indeed, when it was first discovered, it was mistaken as such. An X-ray of the mechanism revealed that instruments of this complexity were not known to exist at least until the 17th century. Who designed and constructed this remarkable device or how this technology was lost afterwards, is not clear. Labeled by scientists as the first mechanical computer in human history, this amazing feat of engineering required that its maker had advanced knowledge of astronomy, as well as a diverse knowledge in mechanics and machine making.

Professor Michael Edmunds of Cardiff University, who led the most recent study of the mechanism, stated that:

> This device is just extraordinary, the only thing of its kind. The design is beautiful, the astronomy is exactly right. The way the mechanics are designed just makes your jaw drop. Whoever has done this has done it extremely carefully...in terms of historic and scarcity value, I have to regard this mechanism as being more valuable than the Mona Lisa. [1]

Another one of the many yet unexplained artifacts that continuously raises eyebrows and stirs many debates among the scientific community, is the famous Baghdad Battery. This primitive version of a modern battery made out of clay vessels, copper tubes, and the right alkaline fluid was capable of producing electricity nearly 2,000 years ago. What was the purpose of the electricity produced by these batteries, and where did this knowledge come from, no one knows. Until their discovery, we were under the impression that battery technology was an 18th century invention.

With every new find, without a doubt, our ancestors continue to demonstrate that several millennia ago they were extremely knowledgeable and more technologically advanced than we have been giving them credit for. How, though, did they come across their incredible knowledge? How could they possess skills that until recently, we thought were acquired during the industrial revolution? Where these really brand new skills, or is it perhaps possible that we evolved much earlier in time and thus developed many of our technological capabilities over the millennia, long before our recorded history? And, if so, if our ancestors truly had advanced thousands of years earlier than anthropologists previously thought, what happened to all past human development?

The story of a "Great Flood" sent by God (or gods according to much earlier testimony) to destroy humanity for its sins is a widespread account shared by many religions and cultures around the world and dates back to our earliest recorded history. From India to ancient Greece, Mesopotamia and even among North American Indian tribes, there is no shortage of such tales that often enough sound very much alike. Some of these stories truly sound so similar that one could wonder whether all cultures around the planet had experienced such an event. Or is it possible they influenced each other by storytelling over the millennia?

Can it be that all flood accounts so zealously repeated around the world are a collection of myths or isolated incidents? Or was the Great Flood a single worldwide cataclysm that affected all humanity at one point during our prehistory? While small isolated disasters can stress and frighten affected populations equally, their overall effect is short-lived, and they often fade from memory within decades, if not years. In the case of the Great Flood, however, we have a story that seems to have no boundaries and one that every culture insists on its worldwide nature. How big and how destructive though, was such a disaster that managed to sear itself into our ancestors' collective memory for thousands of years? Judging by the shared testimony, this must not only have been an event that affected everyone simultaneously, but in order for it to have become a permanent fixture in the human psyche, it must have been an experience that persisted not only for days or months, but for several generations.

Today, although science accepts that regional floods have indeed adversely affected many ancient populations over the millennia, it still denies that there was ever a single deluge that affected every civilization on the planet at once. Meanwhile, while the type, chronology, and magnitude of such an event is still highly debated, several scientific theories of the Great Flood are currently in circulation, and more of them continue to surface from time to time.

In recent years, and according to a published study in 1997 by William Ryan and Walter Pitman, the story of the Great Flood was linked to the "sudden flood" of the Black Sea. According to their hypothesis, at around 5600 BC, the melting of the glaciers—along with several other significant hydrological factors that included the flow of rivers and heavy rainfall—caused the Mediterranean Sea level to rise so rapidly that it ultimately and violently flooded the Black Sea, making it into the body of water we know today.

Ryan and Pitman speculated that the flooding from the Mediterranean occurred via a massive waterfall, nearly two hundred times larger than that of Niagara Falls, which daily dumped ten cubic miles of sea water into the Black Sea for a period of 300 days. By the time it was over, 60,000 square miles around the Black Sea had been submerged. This was the best evidence we had for nearly a decade in order to explain the story of the Great Flood. Although more of a regional flood, undoubtedly, such an event could have utterly destroyed any established civilization around the Black Sea during this period, and rightfully so could have been labeled as a great flood by those who experienced it.

Unfortunately for the Ryan and Pitman team though, another study conducted since reported differently. Although the later research agreed to the premise of the Black Sea being flooded, it contradicted the severity of the flood as well as the chronological time of the event. In 2005, a research project under the sponsorship of UNESCO was conducted by the International Union of Geological Sciences as well as a Ukrainian and Russian scientific team that included Valentina Yanko-Hoback. They published in 2009 that the flood of the Black Sea was more of a gradual event and less catastrophic to human life than previously thought. Most importantly, though, it was determined that the incident took place earlier chronologically, and much closer to 8000 BC. So, in essence, this study confirmed that the flooding of the Black Sea did not have the horrible devastation associated with the loss of human life, and unlike previous estimates, this event definitely took place during our prehistory.

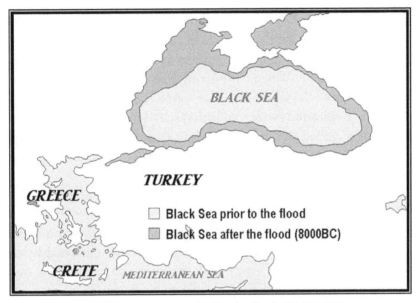

*Black Sea prior to and after the flood of 8000 BC*

If not the flooding of the Black Sea, though, what other regional—or better yet—worldwide catastrophe qualifies to be called the Great Flood? Without a doubt, it was the rise of the oceans at the end of the last ice age. More particularly, it was the abrupt rise of the oceans around 8000 BC which led to the flooding of the Mediterranean first and ultimately to the flooding of the Black Sea. That was the single, long-lasting event which drastically reshaped the coastlines of our planet and the one which simultaneously affected every coastal civilization around the world at the time. In fact, if past periodic ice ages and floods did not manage previously to add salinity into the fresh water of the Black Sea, then undoubtedly the last global flood around 8000 BC must have been the greatest flood of all time.

Although adverse weather conditions, tsunamis, or hurricane-related floods can cause severe destruction several miles inland, the effects from such disasters are always temporary. The significant rise of the oceans, though—a worldwide disaster that erased millions of square miles of dry land around the planet—must have been the doomsday event every culture to this day inadvertently is talking about. Even when at first look, the gradual rise of the oceans does not seem to meet the criteria as the event behind the legend of the Great Flood, an incident responsible for the sea level to rise globally by more than 400 feet, surely had many random episodes when the flooding was absolutely unpredictable. When considering that humans, by nature, tend to settle in lower elevations and near water, it leaves no doubt that all prehistoric civilizations were totally devastated by this event. This must have been a period of constant relocation and adjustment as people continuously kept on looking for higher ground to rebuild and new valleys to grow crops to support those settlements.

To challenge this theory, at least until recently, anthropologists insisted that 10,000 years ago humans were way too primitive to have been aware of such an event. So, in essence, as there were no known civilizations around at the time that could have been affected by this natural catastrophe, the Great Flood story was thought to be a myth or a disaster that have taken place later in time, during our recorded history. Of course, as there are no clues of global cataclysms during our recorded history, this once more led to their eventual conclusion that the Great Flood was either a myth or a much smaller regional incident like the flooding of the Black Sea.

For many years, this was the general "logic" that dominated many academic minds and the greatest challenge to the Ice Age Flood theory, when this hypothesis was brought up.

Incidentally, all this changed in 1994 with the archaeological discovery of Gobekli Tepe, a 12,000-year-old mega site in southeastern Turkey, as well as in 2002 with the discovery of a 10,000-year-old city found submerged under 130 feet of water off the coast of West India in the Gulf of Cambay. In this case, several generations of fishermen insisted on stories of an underwater city in that area, but their claims went unnoticed until the site was accidentally discovered during pollution survey tests conducted by India's National Institute of Ocean

Technology. With the use of side-scan sonar, which sends a beam of sound waves to the bottom of the ocean, scientists found huge geometric structures at the bottom of the sea, at a depth of about 130 feet. Debris recovered from the site, including construction material, pottery, sections of walls, beads, sculptures, and human bones had been carbon dated and found to be approximately 10,000 years old. Scientists now estimate that this 10-square-mile city was sunken after the last ice age, when melting ice 10,000 years ago caused the oceans around the globe to rise significantly. This was an incredible find. Not only does this discovery help rewrite some of the early pages of our history, but most importantly, it confirms ancient testimony in regard to past lost civilizations.

In addition to the ancient city of Jericho, which earlier was established that some of its structures date back to the 10th millennium BC, we now have two additional remarkable discoveries that conclusively prove mankind had advanced much earlier in time than the scientific community was previously aware of. In light of these latest findings, is it possible today to assume that a worldwide flood, roughly 10,000 years ago, may have been the one our ancestors labeled as the Great Flood? Certainly we can. The submerged city off the west coast of India, not only confirms that 10,000 years ago humans were more advanced and thus aware of this particular natural catastrophe, but it further proves that the rising waters, particularly between 8000 BC and 7500 BC, devastated those civilizations and destroyed all evidence of their existence.

In a study published in *Current Anthropology* on December 2010, titled "New Light on Human Prehistory in the Arabo-Persian Gulf Oasis," Jeffrey Rose, an archaeologist and researcher with the United Kingdom's University of Birmingham, pointed out that 60 highly advanced settlements arose out of nowhere around the shores of the Persian Gulf about 7,500 years ago. These settlements featured well-built stone houses, long-distance trade networks, elaborate pottery, and signs of domesticated animals. With no known precursor populations in the archaeological record to explain the existence of these advanced settlements, Rose ultimately concluded the dwellers of these new settlements were those of displaced populations who managed to escape the Gulf inundation around 8000 BC.

As more and more evidence points towards such an assumption, is it so difficult to imagine that such a worldwide cataclysm could have been what erased our early history? If not, how else can we justify the rise of several advanced civilizations around the planet which, since the dawn of our recorded history seem to mysteriously appear out of thin air? Overnight, these people turned out to be masters of architecture, astronomy, and somehow possessed incredible technological skills that neither historians nor anthropologists can quite explain. Is it possible that due to the lack of tangible evidence, early scholars failed to make the connection and to recognize that many of these cultures had advanced thousands of years earlier and prior to the Great Flood? Is it so hard to accept that the incredible megalithic structures and technological achievements of our early recorded history were essentially part of an earlier "renaissance" era that began once the rise of the oceans ended?

Finally, with all clues pointing that more sunken cities around the planet may be awaiting our discovery, can we assume that the rising seas may have been the cataclysm that destroyed yet another great civilization, like that of Atlantis perhaps?

Is it possible that this legendary tale, first mentioned by ancient Egyptians and then written by Plato 2,400 years ago, was true?

According to the Egyptians, not only was Atlantis a real place, but around 9600 BC, the Atlantians were the dominating power around the Mediterranean as they ruled several parts of southern Europe, North Africa, and the Middle East.

Of course, they were not the super-advanced civilization many people during the twentieth century made them out to be, but at best, a civilization more advanced than that of Plato's at the time. Without the technology we possess today, Plato explained that they were extremely innovative as well as capable navigators, who frequently traveled into the Atlantic Ocean to explore.

Today, many theories place Atlantis in locations such as off the coast of southeastern Cyprus, outside the Strait of Gibraltar in the middle of the Atlantic, somewhere in the Bermuda Triangle off the coast of the United States, or even in more exotic locations such as Antarctica or the Pacific Ocean. Of course more mainstream studies point to the tiny island of Santorini, the island of Crete, Malta, Spain, and other archaeological sites around the Mediterranean. Overall, there are countless theories on the location of Atlantis, while more seem to surface every year.

Despite all the scientific and nonscientific speculation though, the vast majority of mainstream scholars today believe that Plato's tale of Atlantis is either a myth, or they assume Plato crafted a story while using a mix of real elements from later times. As for the legendary island, modern historians also tend to think it is not real. Is it possible then that the story of Atlantis was a figment of Plato's imagination? It is certainly possible, although if the story is not real, how can we otherwise explain the real pieces of tangible evidence that seem to corroborate this story?

Of course, the best evidence to prove Atlantis's existence is to find the legendary island itself. Such a discovery would not only validate Plato's claim but would help end the ongoing debate among skeptics and believers. If the island of Atlantis is real, though, why have all past efforts to find it failed? Even if the task to locate a sunken island is not exactly an easy one, when considering our technological capabilities, shouldn't we have been able to find it by now?

From the very beginning, a significant problem in solving this mystery was unquestionably the scientific community's pessimistic position on this subject and their refusal to accept that a 12,000-year-old civilization could have ever been possible. Another huge problem that often complicated the search was our own failure to read and accurately translate Plato's story without allowing personal interpretations to interfere. Finally, when an interpretation was necessary, our failure to be more reasonable in our assumptions made the search even more difficult than it had to be. For example, if (according to Plato) Atlantis was the dominating power around the Mediterranean, shouldn't this revelation lead to the logical assumption that as an island, it should have been somewhere within the Mediterranean as well? On the other hand, the mere mention of another grand island/continent across the Atlantic, outside the Pillars of Hercules (one Plato described as "larger than Libya and Asia put together"), often enough stirs people's imaginations as well as their natural tendencies to chase bigger and better things. This internal drive often causes many people to overlook the smaller tangible clues in the story, and to look for that grand island on the wrong side of the Atlantic. This is akin to the fable of "The Dog and Its Reflection," where a dog is carrying a small bone, looks down as it crosses a stream, and sees its own reflection in the water. Thinking that the reflection was another dog carrying something bigger and better, the dog opens its mouth to grab the larger bone from the "other" dog, and in doing so, drops and loses the bone it was carrying.

Indeed, under close examination, we see that Plato did not really say Atlantis was located on the other side of the Atlantic, but rather he pointed to the fact that the Atlantians were capable of crossing outside the Strait of Gibraltar into the Atlantic Ocean, and travel to all the islands that "encompassed that veritable ocean", including a "grand island", or better yet another continent on the other side of the Atlantic, one that was larger than Libya and Asia combined.

Before attempting to make sense out of a translated document, those not familiar with Greek must know that the syntactic structure of the language that Plato used has a very different structure than the English language we often use to translate it. For example, the simple English phrase "the queen began to talk," translates to Greek as, "began to talk, the queen." What often seems strange to those who first try to learn Greek is the inversion of the possessive adjective in respect to the noun. Similarly, text inversions like these may also exist in the sequence of entire sentences. For example, in an independent clause, an item which is stressed, i.e. which is uttered with emphasis or is contrastive, in ancient Greek generally goes at the beginning of the clause, rarely at the end. The middle position is occupied by an item receiving no particular emphasis. In a series of clauses in a sentence, though, as in the translated text below, a prominent item goes at the beginning of its clause if it relates to the previous context, and at the end if it relates to the following one (the emphasis here, should be placed on the first sentence of the first paragraph, as well as on the last sentence of the second one.)

> **For it is related in our records how once upon a time your State stayed the course of a mighty host,** which, starting from a distant point in the Atlantic ocean, was insolently advancing to attack the whole of Europe, and Asia to boot.

(For) the Ocean that was at that time navigable; for in front of the mouth which you Greeks call, as you say "the Pillars of Hercules" [Strait of Gibraltar] there lay an island which was larger than Libya and Asia together; **and it was possible for travelers of that time to cross from it to the other islands and from the islands to the whole of the continent over against them which encompasses the veritable ocean...** [2]

In this case, and contrary to what many automatically assume, Plato does not point to the direction of Atlantis across the ocean. As explained earlier, the phrase *"your state stayed the course of a mighty host"*, at the beginning of the clause, is where the emphasis first should be placed. While in this sentence, Plato clearly reveals the very close proximity of Atlantis to Greece, in the rest of the sentence he poetically describes the might of Atlantis and its capacity that stretched around the world to a "distant point" and another continent across the ocean. Of course, once he illustrates their incredible capability, he then describes their audacious and warlike character and their plans to "advance against the whole of Europe and Asia".

The same rule applies when analyzing the remaining text. In this case, the revelation of a continent across the ocean is not where the emphasis should be placed. As explained earlier, in a series of clauses in a sentence, prominent items usually are either placed at the beginning or at the end of their clause. The middle part of a sentence is occupied by items that should receive less emphasis. According to this rule, and in this particular case, the explanation of how Atlantians were able to reach the continent across the ocean, at the end of the clause, is where the emphasis should be placed and not on the continent itself that is mentioned earlier (the part that many automatically are drawn to). Not knowing where the emphasis on a clause should be placed, can cause a great deal of confusion as often, and depending where the emphasis goes, two separate meanings can emerge out of a single paragraph. Actually, when it comes to Greek, sometimes even a single comma can cause a short sentence to have two different meanings. Such example is a famous quote from the oracle of Delphi. *"Go, return not die in war"* can have two entirely opposite meanings, depending on where a missing comma is supposed to be - before or after - the word "not."

In short, when a story from ancient Greek is translated to English, the translated sentences may require proper "repositioning" in order for an English reader to make better sense of it. For instance, when understanding the syntactic structure of the Greek language and how to "read it" correctly, Plato's second paragraph above, to an English reader should appear as follows:

> ... and it was possible for travelers of that time to cross from it (the island of Atlantis) to the other islands, and from the islands to the whole of the continent over against them which encompasses the veritable ocean.... (For) the Ocean that was at that time navigable; for in front of the mouth which you Greeks call, as you say "the Pillars of Hercules," there lay a continent which was larger than Libya and Asia together.

When seen in this context, the continent across the ocean is no longer the place of origin for Atlantians, but a destination. Here, Plato simply describes the might of Atlantis by depicting their incredible capability to travel half way around the world. He explains that via island hopping (most likely from Scotland, to the Faroe Islands, to Iceland and then to Greenland), the Atlantians were able to reach another grand island/continent on the other side of the Atlantic, one across from the Pillars of Hercules. Which other continent is on the opposite side of the Atlantic across from the Strait of Gibraltar? The American continent, of course! It was the American continent that Plato said was larger than Libya and Asia put together and not that of Atlantis, as many wrongly had interpreted and even to this day continue to interpret.

As unsettling as it is to some, the revelation that the ancient Greeks knew of the American continent thousands of years before its "discovery" by Christopher Columbus, we must remind ourselves that even much earlier in time they were fully aware that the Earth was round and not flat, as many European civilizations assumed at the time. The Antikythera Mechanism is a testament of such advanced knowledge.

Truly though, around the fourth century BC, it seems that not only did the Greeks know of the American continent, but others did as well, including the Phoenicians and Carthaginians. In 1996, Mark McMenamin, a professor of geology at Mount Holyoke College, discovered and interpreted a series of enigmatic markings on the reverse side of a Carthaginian gold coin, minted circa 350 BC, as an ancient map of the world. In the center of this world map there is a clear depiction of the Mediterranean. An image to the right of it is interpreted to represent Asia, while the image to the left is interpreted to represent the American continent. Professor McMenamin also found that all known specimens of this type of coin formed the same type of "world" map.

This was an interesting discovery, no doubt; however, what is most interesting about this find is that this particular Carthaginian coin was minted within the same decade when Plato unveiled the story of Atlantis and revealed that there was a large continent across from the Pillars of Hercules.

More evidence from around the 4th century BC, though, show that the Carthaginians, along with the Phoenicians and the Greeks, and possibly others, knew of the American continent around that time.

The Piri Reis world map, named after its maker, a Turkish admiral and renowned cartographer (1465-1553), drawn in 1513, merely two decades after the discovery of America by Christopher Columbus, depicts the west coast of Africa, Europe, as well as the entire American continent on the Atlantic side. According to Piri Reis, however, his controversial map was based on several other charts, many dating as early as the 4th century BC!

While by any means the famous map does not come close to a satellite image, still, it properly depicts the continents on both sides of the Atlantic, although with one major flaw. It shows the horn of South America turning sharply eastwards, almost at a 90 degree angle, as if South America "wraps around" the Atlantic at the bottom of the map. While, of course, some go on to speculate that the horizontal body of that land could be that of Antarctica, thus the controversy, since Antarctica was not discovered until 300 years later, skeptics point out that Antarctica was never connected to South America.

Although the controversy in Piri Reis' map significantly diminishes without Antarctica in it, the existence of this map still helps reinforce a couple of assumptions made earlier. If truly Piri Reis borrowed from other ancient maps dating back to the 4th century BC, then unquestionably this reinforces the suggestion that Plato, at 360 BC, could have been aware of the American continent in order to include it in his story. Moreover, is it possible that the apparent flaw on Piri Reis' map, which most likely also appeared on the much older originals, explains why Plato was under the false impression that the immense continent across from the Pillars of Hercules "encompassed" (wrapped around) the Atlantic Ocean?

Additional clues, though, not only hint that the ancient Greeks knew of the large continent across the Atlantic, but as it seems, they were also familiar with the region around the Arctic Circle, in essence the broken bridge that connects northern Europe and North America. They called this land Hyperborea (a Greek word that means "Extremely North".) Is this possible? While undoubtedly skeptics would dismiss this suggestion as an impossible hypothesis, interestingly, the Greeks believed that Hyperborea was an unspoiled territory so far north, the sun there shines 24 hours a day. Of course, the only place due north where the sun continuously shines, at least six months out of a year, is the region above the Arctic circle, a territory obviously not easily accessible, especially during the winter months. Coincidentally, the poet Pindar (522 BC-443 BC) wrote that "neither by ship nor on foot would you find the marvelous road to the assembly of the Hyperboreans," a statement that further corroborates the inaccessibility of this region.

So, when bearing in mind this place's location (somewhere "extremely north",) the fact that is somewhere where the sun never sets, and this is a region inaccessible by foot or boat (most likely due to a frozen Arctic Ocean), where else can a place like this be? Can Hyperborea be the figment of vivid imagination, or is it possible that there is some truth to this story, as in the case of other stories brought to us from ancient Greece, which involved real places wrapped in mythical elements? Such, among others, was the Palace of Knossos, which it was associated with the Minotaur (a mythical beast of half man and half bull,) the city of Troy which was connected with an epic war fought by demigods, and Mount Olympus, which was thought to be occupied by gods. What about Hyperborea though? Is it possible that the Greeks managed to navigate so far north, or was that knowledge passed down to them from others?

If, more than 4000 years ago, according to historians and archae-ologists, the Bronze Age Minoans were often traveling as far as Scotland and the Orkney Islands to trade goods, is it inconceivable to assume that over time they may have reached Greenland (the edge of Hyperborea,) which is couple of short island stops away. Moreover, if those ancient navigators managed to reach Greenland via island hopping, can we further assume that they could have gone a bit further and ultimately found North America, which in essence, is just around the corner? If not, how else could Plato have known that a series of islands ulti-mately connect northern Europe to North America. And consequently, can this fact best explain why Plato was under the impression that the enormous continent across from the Pillars of Hercules "encompassed" (encircled) the Atlantic Ocean?

*From Mediterranean, the route to the Arctic Circle and*
*beyond (known to ancient Greeks as Hyperborea)*

As unbelievable as this revelation may sound to some people, recent evidence, actually, shows that the Minoans, as the Atlantians before them, were regular visitors to the New World. Is this just a coincidence? If both cultures were able to travel to America by following the same exact route, is it also possible to consider that the Atlantians could have been a proto-Minoan culture that collapsed with the rise of the oceans, only later to reform and recommence as a whole new civilization, at least in the eyes of early historians? Is it possible that the rising waters not only washed Atlantis away, but also erased the link that connects these two cultures? Actually, more clues later highlight this connection.

To best visualize how an established civilization can break down, only to re-emerge centuries or millennia later, we must remind ourselves that a single, rather insignificant event by comparison (like the fall of Rome for instance), drove humanity into the dark ages for more than a thousand years. During this period, all past human knowledge somehow seems to have gotten lost, and the earth went from being a sphere to being flat!

When comparing this somewhat negligible incident to that of the rise of the oceans 10,000 years ago (a cataclysm that persisted for centuries and in the process "swallowed" millions of square miles of coastal land and, along with it, all human development), then is easy to understand the force that literally erased our early history.

A recent study published in *Science News* (December 4, 2010) titled "Global Sea-Level Rise at the End of the Last Ice Age Interrupted by Rapid Jumps" better explains that after the end of the last ice age, from around 17000 BC through 4000 BC, sea levels (on average) rose by one meter per century. However, the study also indicated that this gradual rise of the seas was marked by abrupt jumps of sea level at a rate of about five meters per century. More precisely, the study showed that the periods between 13000 BC and 11000 BC, as well as between 9000 BC and 7000 BC, were characterized by abnormal sea-level rise.

When studying closer the abrupt climatic changes during the last 18,000 years, the time between 9000 BC and 7000 BC is of particular interest. As the glaciers began to melt over thousands of years prior to this period, and the temperatures progressively began to increase with each passing century, thus causing the melting process to accelerate, we can easily presume that this must have been the most active period in sea-level rise. More accurately, the absolute worst period must have been the time around 8000 BC and the critical "flood cycle" that preceded the flooding of the Black Sea, which really marked the end of this violent period.

About this time, in addition to the glacier meltwater that heavily flowed into the Atlantic, two enormous glacial lakes in North America burst open, first Lake Agassiz and later Lake Ojibway, and began to drain into the northern Atlantic. Lake Agassiz alone, covering an area larger than all of the modern Great Lakes combined (440,000 square kilometers), at times it contained more water than all the lakes in the world today. It is estimated that the outburst flood caused by the collapse of Lake Agassiz alone may have been responsible for sea levels to rise globally by as much as nine feet. The total fresh water outflow from both lakes was so immense that not only quickly raised sea levels worldwide by several feet, but this incident may have ultimately caused the "8.2 kilo-year event" that followed approximately 8,200 years ago (a mini ice age that lasted up to four centuries).

It was during this period when most coastal civilizations around the planet were lost, including the sunken city in India and that of Atlantis. The continuous, rapid rise of the sea during this period (by an average of 20 to 30 feet per century or more), along with the adverse climatic conditions that accompanied this phenomenon, made it impossible for the remnants of any civilization to reestablish itself.

Only after 7000 BC when the ocean levels finally began stabilizing, human life once more began to return to normal. Coastal sites no longer had to be abandoned for higher ground, at least for the most part, and between 6000 BC and 5000 BC, once more, we begin to see signs of human activity closer to the sea. Is it a mere coincidence that our "recorded" history happens to start around this time? Is it true that early humans were too primitive to leave traces of their existence behind, or were the early pages of our history "washed away" by the Great Flood of the last ice age? After all, it seems that as soon as the adverse climatic conditions receded, it did not take long for humans to thrive once again. The Atlantians, now called the Minoans by modern historians, reacquired their old abilities and quickly became the great seafaring civilization they once were. Once again, they began to travel and trade outside the Mediterranean and went as far as the Americas, as some archaeological evidence shows.

Indeed, several clues in North America as well as on the island of Santorini, confirm that during the Bronze Age the Minoans were not only heavily mining copper from the area around Lake Superior, but they were regularly carrying tobacco and other spices from the Americas back to Santorini. Many ancient copper mines around the Great Lakes and primarily in the upper peninsula of Michigan are a testament of those days. More than 5,000 shallow mines, up to 20 feet in depth, were discovered just within an area roughly 200 kilometers long by 10 kilometers wide. Carbon dating of artifacts found around these mines indicates that the mines were active during the Bronze Age, between 2470 BC and 1050 BC. Even more surprisingly, a carbon 14 testing of wood remains found inside sockets of copper artifacts on Isle Royale, and on nearby Keweenaw Peninsula (a region filled with copper mine pits), indicated that some mines in that area were in use between 3700 BC and 5000 BC, if not earlier.

A conservative estimate indicates that around 3000 BC, as many as 500,000 tons of copper were extracted from the upper peninsula of Michigan, an undertaking that cannot be clearly explained by mainstream historians or archaeologists. Not only no one in the New World at that time could have extracted and used the copper, but no significant copper remnants were ever found in the Americas to account for the missing ore. So, while today's researchers theorize that some ancient European civilization may have been the one to have utilized the precious metal, the only Bronze Age culture at the time capable of navigating to the Americas were the post-Atlantian Minoans.

More evidence, however, ties the Minoans to the New World. Ancient tools left behind around Lake Superior match those of the Minoans found in other European mines. Also, the type of copper extracted from North America, when chemically tested, closely matches the Minoan product.

Evidence that connects the Minoans to the Americas, though, also exists on the island of Santorini. Archaeological excavations on the island revealed that the Minoans were also importing tobacco from North America. More precisely, an excavation in the ancient city of Akrotiri, near what was a merchant's house, revealed that a tobacco beetle indigenous to America was buried under the volcanic ash of the 1600 BC eruption. As the tobacco beetle, *Lasioderma serricorne*, was indigenous only to America at the time, and historically tobacco was not introduced to Europeans until around 1518 AD (nearly 3,000 years later), this find further reinforces the suggestion that the Minoans could have been importing tobacco along with copper from the New World.

Of course this revelation solves yet another historical puzzle. How, during this period, ancient Egyptians obtained tobacco and other spices indigenous to America. Several early tests on Egyptian mummies revealed that some of the plants and spices, including tobacco, used during the mummification process were indigenous to Central America. Interestingly, the same type of beetle that was discovered in Santorini, a sort of "pest of stored tobacco," was also found inside the mummy of Ramses II (1213 BC) and inside King Tutankhamen's tomb (1323 BC).

In 1992, more tests by German scientists on several mummies exposed remnants of hashish, tobacco, and cocaine on their hair, skin, and bones. The results were a huge surprise, to say the least. Unlike the hashish that historically originates in Asia, tobacco and coca were strictly New World plants at the time of mummification. In order to be sure that the results were not tainted somehow, or most likely, to allow themselves to step outside this controversial discovery, the German team hired an independent lab to redo these particular tests. Needless to say, the independent lab found precisely the same substances. Out of the hundreds of mummies they tested, including that of Ramses II, they found nicotine traces on at least a third of them. This discovery leaves no doubt that not only the ancient Egyptians were in need of a large supply of tobacco, but as it appears, the enterprising Minoans were regularly supplying them with it.

The best evidence to connect the Minoans to the Americas, though, doesn't come to us in the form of copper, tobacco, and other plants, but in the form of DNA. In fact, DNA analysis shows that in their endeavors to the Americas, the Atlantians first (and later the Minoans) left their genetic fingerprint behind.

For the longest time, geneticists wondered and debated how haplogroup X, a Mediterranean gene, migrated to America thousands of years before the American continent was discovered by the Europeans.

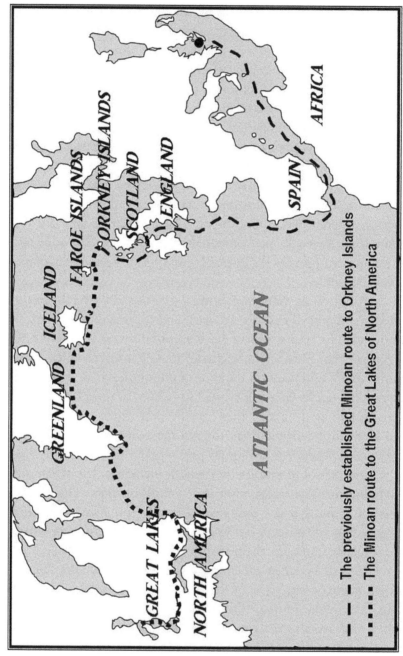

*The Minoan route to North America during the Bronze Age.
According to Plato, at around 9600BC, the Atlantians
used the same route to reach North America.*

More specifically, how did some tribes in North America, and suspiciously those that originated around the Great Lakes, like the Ojibwa (known also as Chippewa) Indians, found to carry this particular gene while other tribes further away didn't?

The mystery deepened when scientists suggested that the Mediterranean haplogroup X somehow could have "mutated" among the North American tribes as early as 10,000 to 12,000 years ago.

For those not familiar with genetics, each race around the planet is categorized by scientists according to their particular DNA haplogroup. For example, all American Indians contain haplogroups A, B, C, and D. As haplogroups A, C, and D are also found primarily in Asia, and B mainly in China and Japan, it is highly speculated by anthropologists that these four haplogroups traveled to North America during a glacier period when continents were once connected by ice. A more recent study, though, on certain Native American tribes like the Iroquois Indians and a few others, revealed that in addition to the above haplogroups that scientists had expected to find, they were also found to carry haplogroup X. This discovery came as a big surprise because haplogroup X originates from an area that incorporates the eastern Mediterranean, the Palestinian territories, Syria, Jordan, Lebanon, Cyprus, Israel and northeast Africa.

If Middle Easterners somehow made it to America 10,000 years ago, why did only tribes around the Great Lakes carry this particular gene? And most importantly, how did Mediterranean people manage the trip to North America? Is it possible, as the majority of anthropologists suggest, that 10,000 years ago they traveled to America while ice still connected the Asian and American continents at the Bering Strait? After all, as we are told, this is how haplogroups A, B, C, and D crossed over to the Americas. A huge problem with this theory though, is that en route from the Middle East to America, the furthest region east of the Mediterranean to carry small traces of haplogroup X is that of the Altai Republic in Russia. No traces of haplogroup X (or another variation of X) exist further east of that region. And, while the majority of scientists continue to hold onto the Bering Strait hypothesis, no one can provide a conclusive explanation for the lack of haplogroup X in the enormous void between southern Russia and the greater region of the Great Lakes.

Of course, there are those who support an earlier theory, called the Solutrean/Clovis hypothesis, which suggests the crossing was not made through the Bering Strait, but instead, Europeans crossed over to America on an ice sheet that partially connected Europe with North America. Oddly enough, this scenario suggests that out of the ten distinct haplogroups present in northern Europe at the time (H, V, J, HV, U, T, UK, X, W, and I), conveniently, only haplogroup X managed the trip to America. The model in this hypothesis also required that the early travelers, over 10,000 years ago, crossed over to the Americas in small watercrafts constructed out of animal skins and used survival skills similar to those of Inuit people, not exactly the trades of a Mediterranean culture. Considering all this, it is no wonder that another study done in 2008, using relevant oceanographic data, pointed out that the conditions for such a crossing were not favorable, and the Solutrean hypothesis was afterwards dismissed by the majority of scientists. Therefore, the mystery of how haplogroup X made it to North America still remains.

If somehow the path to America was open from either direction (the Bering Strait or the North Atlantic), and any European gene could follow haplogroup X to the New World, how do we explain that only one Caucasian/Mediterranean gene (out of at least a dozen) made this trip 10,000 years ago, while on the opposite side every one of the four Asian haplogroups sequentially managed to follow each other to America through the Bering Strait? Conversely, though, if haplogroup X did not enter the American continent via the Atlantic, as most anthropologists continue to maintain, how do we explain the fact that elevated concentrations of haplogroup X also "strangely" exist in Scotland, Faroe Islands and Iceland, essentially all the "island stops" on the way to North America from Europe. We must also not ignore that mtDNA maps show that the highest concentrations of haplogroup X exist on the Atlantic side, around the Great Lakes, and not in Alaska or alongside the west coast where according to science haplogroup X infiltrated America.

Before allowing for religious beliefs to become reasonable theories, like the Mormon hypothesis which claims 10,000 years ago, Israelites "appeared" in America with God's "assistance," is it time perhaps to give Plato's story another closer look?

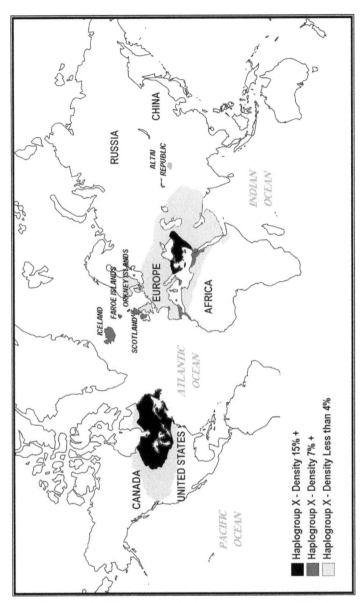

*According to mtDNA maps, the highest concentration of haplogroup X away from the eastern Mediterranean (the place of origin for haplogroup X) is found around the Great Lakes of North America. Incidentally, high traces of haplogroup X also exist around the Strait of Gibraltar, Scotland, Orkney Islands, Faroe islands, and Iceland.*

**For all that we have here, lying within the mouth of which we speak, is evidently a haven having a narrow entrance;** but that yonder is a real ocean, and the land surrounding it may most rightly be called, in the fullest and truest sense, a continent. **Now in this island of Atlantis there existed a confederation of kings, of great and marvelous power, which held sway over all the island, and over many other islands also and parts of the continent.** [3]

Once more and as previously explained, the main emphasis in this case must be placed on the first as well as the last sentence of the paragraph. While these two sentences convey the topic, the middle sentence in this case provides the supporting details.

In this paragraph, Plato clearly depicts Atlantis as an idyllic place with a narrow entrance somewhere within the Mediterranean Sea (lying within the mouth of which we speak.) He then explains that the mighty Atlantians not only had power over their own island, but they controlled parts of the large continent across the ocean, including several other islands. The second sentence, the supporting sentence in this case, further clarifies that the large continent across the Atlantic was that of America, and the islands they held sway over were obviously the islands that allowed them to get there (the Orkney islands, Faroe Islands, Iceland, etc.)

When comparing Plato's account to the map above, is there a doubt that he offers yet the most convincing explanation how haplogroup X migrated to the New World, and why heavy traces of X also exist on every island stop from Europe to the Great Lakes of North America.

While, without a doubt, this explanation in comparison to others, seems to be more plausible, we must not ignore that when the original human migration scenarios were first proposed, in order to best explain the presence of haplogroup X in America, the mainstream academia assumed that 10,000 years ago humans were still behaving as hunters and gatherers. With that in mind, it is no wonder that Plato's story was immediately dismissed as a myth.

Recent archaeological discoveries, however, like that of Gobekli Tepe in Turkey (10000 BC) and the sunken city off the coast of West India (8000 BC), not only proved that humans had advanced much earlier in time, but they could have plausibly reached North America. Unlike other mainstream theories, Plato's story not only places haplogroup X in America in the right chronology, but explains how, in a contained environment it arrived at the Great Lakes. By the way, let us not forget that 10,000 years ago, with the ocean levels at least 400 feet lower, there was so much more landmass between Scotland, Iceland, and Greenland that island hopping to North America could not have been more difficult than crisscrossing the Mediterranean. Any competent prehistoric Mediterranean navigator, who could travel as far as Scotland, ultimately could have developed the skills to navigate all the way to North America.

Still, as difficult as it is for some to accept that thousands of years ago a Mediterranean culture discovered the New World, physical evidence further confirms that a Caucasian race visited North America several millennia ago.

The Kennewick Man is the name given to the skeletal remains of a prehistoric man found on a bank of the Columbia River in Kennewick, Washington, on July 28, 1996. The skull was accidentally discovered by Will Thomas and David Deacy while they were attending an annual event. Later, a team of professionals was able to recover 350 additional skeletal pieces, thus making the Kennewick Man the most complete prehistoric skeleton ever found. Interestingly, while scientists at first thought the remains belonged to a Native Indian from the nineteenth century, a radiocarbon dating conducted by the University of California at Riverside concluded that the skeleton was approximately 9800 years old. Even more incredibly, when forensic archaeologist James Chatters further studied the bones and especially the cranium features of the skeleton, he concluded that they belonged to a Caucasoid male about sixty-eight inches (or 173 centimeters) tall.

> The man lacks definitive characteristics of the classic mongoloid stock to which modern Native Americans belong. The skull is dolichocranic (cranial index 73.8) rather than brachycranic, the face narrow and progna-

thous rather than broad and flat. Cheek bones recede slightly and lack an inferior zygomatic projection; the lower rim of the orbit is even with the upper. Other features are a long, broad nose that projects markedly from the face and high, round orbits. The mandible is v-shaped, with a pronounced, deep chin. Many of these characteristics are definitive of modern-day Caucasoid peoples, while others, such as the orbits are typical of neither race. [4] (Chatters, J.)

The mystery deepened when Dr. Chatters discovered a stone projectile lodged in the Ilium (part of the pelvic bone), which had partially grown around it. Interestingly, under a CT scan, it was revealed that the leaf-shaped projectile itself was from a siliceous grey stone that was found to have intrusive volcanic origins. As Atlantis was reportedly characterized by black (dark grey), red, and white volcanic material, is it possible that this projectile originated from that particular environment?

Unfortunately, when DNA was extracted from the skeleton in order to determine—once and for all—the origin and race of the remains, the scientists who were performing the DNA analysis announced that, "Available technology and protocols do not allow the analysis of ancient DNA from these remains."

Additional studies were conducted to determine the origin of the Kennewick Man, with some speculating he must have been of an Asian ancestry. More recent work on the remains by Douglas Owsley, though, a physical anthropologist at the Smithsonian Institution's National Museum of History, further concluded that the Kennewick Man's ancestors did not originate in northern Asia like those of most Native Americans who are believed to have crossed from Asia to Alaska about 11,000 years ago.

Even when comparing the skull of Kennewick Man to a typical Polynesian skull (as some theorize Polynesia may have been his place of origin), certain cranium features, like the lower jaw bone, nonetheless support the initial diagnosis that the remains belong to a Caucasian. Yet, if the Kennewick Man was ultimately found to be Polynesian, his presence in North America still substantiates Plato's claim that ten millennia ago, it was also possible for an advanced Mediterranean culture to navigate to the New World. Clearly, following the longer coastline from Polynesia to North America, presents by far a greater challenge than crossing over to the Americas from Europe via the north Atlantic.

In essence, the Kennewick Man's remarkable discovery not only confirms that it was possible for prehistoric humans to travel to the New World 10,000 years ago, but this find further supports Plato's story and reinforces the possibility that not only the Atlantians could have made it to North America, but in time they could have been followed by their successors—the Minoans. Of course, the Minoan presence in America during the Bronze Age, not only helps account for the missing copper around Lake Superior, but also can explain the Caucasian "sightings" in Central America reported by the Mayan Indians.

The Mayans, one of Central America's greatest and most mysterious civilizations, were established around 2000 BC, and are known to have been the dominating power in the region of Central America for more than two millennia. While, on the surface, we know them to be expert architects and masters of astronomy, in truth, very little is known about these people and their civilization. Author Charles Gallenkamp, in his book *Maya: The Riddle and Rediscovery of a Lost Civilization*, wrote,

> Regardless of everything scientists have learned about the Maya so far, we constantly encounter unanswered questions. No one has satisfactory explained where or when Maya civilization originated, or how it evolved in an environment so hostile to human habitation. We have almost no reliable information on the origin of their calendar, hieroglyphic writing, and mathematical system; nor do we understand countless details pertaining to sociopolitical organization, religion, economic structure, and everyday life. Even the shattering catastrophe leading to the sudden abandonment of their greatest cities during the ninth century AD—one of the most baffling archaeological mysteries ever uncovered—is still deeply shrouded in conjecture. [5]

Chronologically, the Mayan civilization emerged during the Bronze Age and at the time when copper around Lake Superior was heavily mined by the Minoans. Is this timing just an unrelated coincidence or a clue worth following?

While the Mayans are not known to have traveled as far north as Lake Superior, thus never before had they seen a Caucasian man, interestingly they depict their god, Kukulkan, as a Caucasian person with white hair, standing about six feet tall. The Mayans further explain that Kukulkan came from the sea, and when it was time for him to leave, once again he departed back to the sea with a promise that one day he would return.

According to the Mayans, Kukulkan taught them how to organize and manage their civilization, and (among other skills) taught them agriculture, medicine, and architecture. Who Kukulkan was and why the Mayans portrayed him as a white man is anyone's guess. Or is there an explanation for that? Is it possible that Kukulkan was a Bronze Age visitor to the Great Lakes who in search of more wealth and opportunity, may have traveled farther south to Central America and ultimately helped or inspired the local tribes to organize? Certainly, Kukulcan's arrival from the sea and his personal appearance is highly suspicious.

If not a Bronze Age visitor though, who was this Caucasian person that the Mayans attributed their culture to? Although no one will ever know for sure, one thing is certain: when the Mayans met the Spanish conquistadors for the "first time," not only did they mistake them for gods, but they thought the Spanish arrival was the return of Kukulkan. Once again, why would the Mayans think the European settlers were gods? Is it possible that an earlier Minoan visit had something to do with that presumption?

Actually, if the Minoans were traveling back and forth to North America for more than a thousand years, is there any doubt that they could have traveled further south until ultimately they reached Central America? Some evidence, as well as Mayan testimony, confirms this suggestion.

In 1966, Manfred Metcalf, a civilian employee of Fort Benning in Georgia, was gathering stones for a barbeque pit when he discovered a flat, square-shaped, five-pound stone with strange symbols engraved on it. This rock was later named the Metcalf Stone.

Thinking that the symbols on the stone could have been some form of Indian writing, Mr. Metcalf presented the stone to Dr. Joseph Mahan Jr., an expert in Yuchi Indian dialect and director of the Columbus Museum of Arts and Crafts. When the stone was presented to him, Dr. Mahan had been primarily studying the Yuchi Indians, a tribe in the region that was racially and linguistically different from all other Indians in North America.

In 1968, when Dr. Mahan completed his studies on the stone, he forwarded a cast copy to Cyrus Gordon at Brandeis University. To everyone's surprise, Mr. Gordon concluded that the markings on the stone matched characters used by the Minoans 3,500 years earlier on the island of Crete.

In effect, the Metcalf Stone not only reinforces the notion that the Bronze Age Minoans traveled as far south as the state of Georgia but also raises a valid question of whether there is a connection between the Minoans and the Yuchi Indians in the area, a tribe of "Indians" like no other. Furthermore, the Minoan presence in the southeastern United States also tends to suggest that the Minoans may have traveled farther south and maybe all the way to Central America—not just once, but repeatedly.

An ancient Yucatan manuscript from the town of Motul further supports this assumption. It describes a time when the Mayans worshipped a heavenly god and creator of all things until a long-bearded Caucasian prince named Kukulkan arrived from the sea. Contrary to earlier Mayan religious beliefs and practices, it was he who brought the "dark side" to their civilization. In his book *Fair Gods and Feathered Serpents*, T.J. O'Brien noted the following:

> Originally a god had been worshiped here who was the creator of all things, and who had his dwelling in heaven, but that great prince named Kukulkan with a multitude of people had come from a foreign country, that he and his people were idolaters, and from that time the inhabitants of this land also began to practice idolatry, to perform bloody sacrificial rites, to burn copal, and the like. [6]

Kukulkan and his "multitude of people" (his crew-mates, per-haps?) were idol worshippers, and he frequently commanded sacrificial ceremonies to be enacted in his name. Among other bizarre sacrifices, he often asked that young virgins be thrown 65 feet down into the water well of Chichen Itza in order to take messages to the gods of the underworld. During the twentieth century when the well was dredged, researchers found several remains of women, children, and men whose bodies had been discarded in the huge well.

The same manuscript further explains that even after the long-bearded man's departure, the Mayans continued to build temples to his name and perform human sacrifices to honor him. Strangely, many figures of bearded men, an uncommon facial characteristic among Central American Indians, were also carved in various stone monu-ments, including one on the wall of Chichen Itza's ball court. Who was this bearded man? Is it possible that Kukulkan was a Minoan perpetra-tor who demanded human offerings? And if so, were the Minoans at all known to have practiced human sacrifices? Surprisingly, the answer is yes. Recent archaeological excavations and evidence from three dif-ferent sites on the island of Crete suggest that the Minoans indeed sacrificed humans. The three sites are Anemospilia, in a building near Mount Juktas that is interpreted as a temple; in a sanctuary complex at Fournou Korifi in South-central Crete; and at Knossos, in a building known as the North House.

So, if the Minoans made it to Central America, and in the pro-cess they were mistaken as gods, is it possible then to assume that the dreadful tradition which plagued the Mayan civilization could have been a tradition that was actually introduced to them by another cul-ture (and vice versa)? Is it possible that some Mayan traditions and/or objects from Central America were taken back to Crete and displayed by the Minoans as well? For example, under a closer examination, the elaborate headpiece with the long colorful feathers in a famous Minoan fresco (named "Prince of Lilies") could be, in effect, a depiction of a "souvenir" brought back from the New World. If anything, it pro-foundly resembles a helmet piece usually worn by Mayan priests rather than Minoan royalty. While traditionally we see similar headgear as a standard piece of attire in Mayan art, this distinct piece will not be seen again in other Minoan illustrations. More particularly, all other head pieces depicted in Minoan art appear to be slim, elegant, and ring-like hair straps. Is it possible, then, that this particular headpiece could be of Mayan origin? Was it a trophy perhaps brought from the New World?

*On the left, a depiction of a Mayan priest with a typical headdress and attire (a 1787 illustration by Richardo Almendariz of a stucco relief at Palenque). On the right, a Minoan fresco from Crete (labeled by archeologists as the "prince of lilies") features a nearly identical headdress. The long feathers are identical, the material which covers the helmet itself appear to be woven in the same fashion, and in front of the helmet, as on the Mayan headpiece, there is an ornament that leaps out forward.*

Soon after the Minoan demise at around 1500 BC, various artifacts and inscriptions from other Middle Eastern cultures found in North America actually confirm that others eventually took notice and ultimately followed the Minoan footsteps to the Americas. It is believed that the Mycenaean Greeks, along with the Phoenicians, followed the Minoans next. Just as the Minoans, the Greeks also left behind their own small relics and other clues to reveal their presence in the New World.

The fact that the most western island of Faroe Islands still bears the name "Mykines" (Mycenae in Greek), implies that the Mycenaean

Greeks, as the Atlantians and Minoans before them, may have indeed visited North America via island hopping. By the way, out of four island stops, this was the second stop on the way to North America from Scotland.

After the Mycenaean Greeks, the Phoenicians, who came to the New World just a few centuries after the Minoans, were also an enterprising maritime trading culture that thrived around the Eastern Mediterranean between 1500 BC and 300 BC. Very much like the Minoans, they were capable of traveling outside the Strait of Gibraltar, where they usually traded goods as far as the Azores Islands and alongside the African coast on the Atlantic side. The Phoenicians are also known to have circumnavigated Africa, so for them, a trip to America via "island hopping" would not be an improbable suggestion. Indeed, inscriptions found in North America validate the hypothesis that the Phoenicians made it to the New World, and it is possible that they came in contact with the Mayans while there.

The Bat Creek Stone, found in a burial mound in Tennessee, was inscribed with Paleo-Hebrew lettering and dates between the first and second centuries AD. Another exciting find that places the Phoenicians in the Americas is the petroglyphs inscribed on the Dighton Rock found in Berkley, Massachusetts. In 1783, Ezra Stiles, then president of Yale College, identified the writing on Dighton Rock as being Hebrew—a language also commonly used by the Phoenicians. The Phoenicians and Israelites at the time were cohabitants of the land of Canaan and were so closely intertwined they often intermarried and worshipped common Canaanite gods.

Is it possible that the Minoan and most importantly the Phoenician presence in the southeastern United States, can explain why some Indian tribes in this region, like the Cherokee for example, proclaim Jewish genealogy? Although initially those claims and beliefs were highly questioned by skeptics, it is worth to mention that recent DNA tests revealed that Cherokee roots include Egyptian, Greek, Phoenician, as well as Hebrew lineages.

Just as in the case of Cherokee Indians, is it possible to assume that in their endeavors at the new World, prior to their own demise, the Minoans met and helped the Mayan establish their civilization? And, can we further assume that few centuries later, another Middle

Eastern culture, the Phoenicians perhaps, offered their own contribution. And, if not the Minoans, could the Phoenicians be the white, long-bearded men the Mayans talked about? Lastly, does this alleged interaction in any way explain why Mayan architecture appears to be a hybrid of Minoan and Mesopotamian structures? While several Mayan buildings undoubtedly carry Minoan features and characteristics, the Mayans (and later the Aztecs) are also known for their step pyramids, an architectural element that best matches Middle Eastern architecture, especially the ziggurats of ancient Mesopotamia. Maybe a Phoenician influence could best explain that. In his 1871 book *Ancient America*, John Denison Baldwin wrote,

> The known enterprise of the Phoenician race, and this ancient knowledge of America, so variously expressed, strongly encourage the hypothesis that the people called Phoenicians came to this continent, established colonies in the region where ruined cities are found, and filled it with civilized life. It is argued that they made voyages on the "great exterior ocean," and that such navigators must have crossed the Atlantic; and it is added that symbolic devices similar to those of the Phoenicians are found in the American ruins, and that an old tradition of the native Mexicans and Central Americans described the first civilizers as "bearded white men," who "came from the East in ships." [7]

It seems that John Denison Baldwin was on to something when he first suggested that Phoenicians visited America. Certainly, the depiction of the long-bearded Caucasian man carved on the ball-court wall at Chichen Itza, if not of a Minoan ancestry, it appears to be that of a Middle Eastern person.

While the Minoans and Phoenicians may be those behind the enigmatic maps of antiquity, and their presence in Central America explains some of the architectural and other characteristics the Mayans shared with these two cultures, when comparing the Minoan civilization to that of Atlantis, the similarities are so striking that it raises a valid question of whether these two societies, separated by few millennia, were actually one and the same.

For instance, just as the Atlantians before them, we know the Minoans were a mercantile society heavily involved in "global" trade. Both are known to have regularly traveled outside the Strait of Gibraltar, and both reportedly reached the American continent via the same route. Both the Atlantians and the Minoans had a formidable navy that not only helped them to rule the Mediterranean but ensured that their coastal colonies remained safe. Both civilizations lived in unfortified cities, and both relied on their powerful navy for protection. This further indicates that both were island civilizations as they had no fear of land invasion. Both seem to have practiced the same religion with the bull being their primary idol.

Although chronologically both cultures are separated by nearly three millennia, both employed technologies ahead of their time and utilized similar architecture that was characterized by red, white, and black building material. Finally, and most importantly, both civilizations derived from within the same region. In fact, a common ground that physically connects the two cultures, and ultimately brings the two civilizations closer together, is the small island of Santorini.

While Santorini is known historically as a Minoan settlement, the island's makeup of red, black, and white volcanic material physically matches Plato's description and location of where the city of Atlantis once stood. More importantly, though, in addition to the island's natural composition, the physical shape of Santorini, which contains an island within an island, provides another striking resemblance. Does that mean Santorini itself may be Plato's lost island of Atlantis? Some would argue with this suggestion. While Santorini may perfectly match Atlantis's capital site, the island itself is too small to be the "grand island" of Atlantis. Also, neither Santorini nor the island of Crete (150 kilometers away), which some speculate was the primary island of Atlantis, matches Plato's physical description.

But if the small island of Santorini provides sound evidence that it once was the site to the capital city of Atlantis, where then is the primary island, and how does Santorini fit into Plato's story? Moreover, is it possible that the enigmatic and highly advanced Minoans were a post-Atlantian culture?

According to historians, the Minoans were a Bronze Age civilization that arose on the island of Crete and flourished from the twenty-seventh to the fifteenth century BC. Various artifacts and signs of advanced agriculture on Crete, though, dating as far back as 5000 BC, point to a much earlier Minoan presence on the island. Are those signs really from the Minoans, or do they belong to another much older civilization like that of Atlantis perhaps? Is it possible that the two cultures were one and the same, only to be separated by time during the rise of the oceans? Obviously if the two were established and thrived over the same region in two separate time periods, it would be extremely difficult to tell them apart.

Archaeologists actually had a similar challenge when they first discovered and debated the Sumerian and Babylonian artifacts. In that particular case, as the language was nearly identical, it took decades to separate who was who before finally realizing that the Sumerians preceded the Babylonians by at least 2,000 years.

So if archaeologists are now placing the Minoan presence in the region as far back as the sixth millennium BC, is it possible perhaps that one day we will discover that this "Minoan presence" goes even further back to the eighth or even ninth millennium BC? And if so, could those archaeological remnants really be Minoan, or maybe those of Atlantis? Clearly, without first discovering the lost island nearby, it will be extremely difficult to prove that a 10,000-year-old civilization in the area could be that of Atlantis. Unfortunately, though, while we are searching for more tangible clues, we must not ignore that the fate of Atlantis itself may also be an indicator as to what happened to the rest of the physical evidence.

So, what really do we know of Atlantis that could help in its discovery? According to Plato, he was repeating a story first revealed to Greek lawmaker, Solon, by Egyptian priests during one of his visits to Egypt. The Egyptians told Solon that, at around 9600 BC, Atlantis was a mighty naval empire that ruled many parts of southern Europe, North Africa, and the Middle East.

In 360 BC, in the dialogues of *Timaeus and Critias*, Plato described Atlantis in much broader detail. In *Critias*, Plato clearly depicted Atlantis as an island with its northern portion consisting mostly of mountains that reached the shores. Just south of this mountainous region, he said there was a great oblong valley that measured 3,000 stadia (roughly 555 square kilometers). Farther south, and closer to the center of the island, a smaller valley encircled by low-rise mountains measured 2,000 stadia (roughly 370 square kilometers). Fifty stadia from the coast and south of the main island (about nine kilometers away) there was a small circular island. In the flooded center of this round island there was a tiny island measuring about five stadia in diameter (about 0.92 kilometers).

This setting of an island within an island, which undoubtedly resembles the locale of a sea volcano with a collapsed core, was the location where the crown city of Atlantis once stood. Various bridges connected the tiny inner island to the cliffs of the outer island. A single narrow opening on the outer ring of cliffs allowed for ships to enter the port of Atlantis in the center of the island. This detail further reveals that the outer cliffs that encircled the city center were actually surrounded by water, a detail which further proves that the crown city of Atlantis was an island itself.

In his account, Plato further depicted Atlantians as great architects and innovators that were involved in mass-scale agriculture. As he explained, irrigation to support the island's crops was produced by large water canals located in the central valley of the main island, while the mountains surrounding this central valley provided additional fresh water as well as timber for construction. There was an abundance of minerals on the island including orichalcum, a particular type of copper, which at the time was the most valuable metal next to gold. In addition to domesticated animals, there were many wild animals on the grand island of Atlantis, including numerous elephants.

According to Plato, Atlantis was ultimately lost to the sea in a "single day and night of misfortune."

Today, due to the striking resemblance of Santorini to Plato's city of Atlantis, and the fact that the mysterious Minoan civilization appears to have many similarities with that of Atlantis, have some historians speculating that the Minoan civilization and Santorini itself must have been Plato's Atlantis. The concentric rings of earth and water around the center of the city, without a doubt, highly resemble the physical description of Santorini.

Another detail in Plato's description that further links Santorini to Atlantis was the presence of two natural springs, one of cold and one of hot water. Of course, as the origin of the hot water was clearly geothermic, this further suggests that the island of Atlantis must have been volcanic, just as Santorini is.

> The two springs, cold and hot, provided unlimited sup-
> ply of water for appropriate purposes, remarkable for its
> agreeable quality and excellence... [8]

As previously mentioned, ongoing archaeological excavations on the island of Santorini, and particularly at the city of Akrotiri, revealed that the 4,000-year-old city, fitted with sewers, had an elaborate supply system of hot and cold water.

Those not familiar with Santorini should know that the entire island is a massive volcano with a collapsed center. The huge crater in the center of the island, about 12 kilometers wide at its widest part, is flooded with seawater and today serves as the island's idyllic port. In the center of this watery crater, there is a tiny uninhabited island that allows Santorini to match Plato's description. Based on its striking resemblance, volcanic composition and other similarities, is it possible to assume that Santorini may have been the location where the crown city of Atlantis once stood? Many skeptics disagree, saying the massive volcanic eruption of 1600 BC must have hugely altered the shape of this island. Several geological studies and other recent conclusions, though, point to quite the opposite. Surprisingly, it appears that the pre-eruption Santorini resembled Plato's city of Atlantis site even more.

In 1991, it was established by Druitt and Francaviglia that the ancient island of Santorini was made of concentric rings of land and sea even before the eruption. In fact, there is only one significant difference between the modern and prehistoric Santorini. It was determined that the outer ring of the caldera that currently makes the primary island was nearly solid, with only a single opening to allow ship access into the watery center of the island. Today, the post-eruption Santorini has three openings that allow ships to enter into the watery caldera. Moreover, the small island in the center of the caldera, prior to the eruption of Santorini 3,600 years ago, was a much bigger island—large enough to match Plato's description and to hold the entire city center along with the temple of Poseidon.

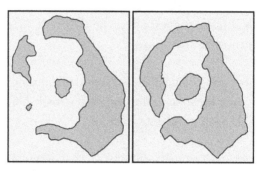

*The island of Santorini, present day (left).*
*The island of Santorini prior to the volcanic eruption of 1600BC,*
*according to a 1991 study by Druitt and Francaviglia (right).*

It is worth to mention that the volcanic eruption of Santorini, 3,600 years ago, was the second largest, if not the largest, in recorded history. The explosion was so intense that not only 60 cubic kilometers of magma and rock is estimated to have erupted from the volcano, but the event created several tsunamis of unimaginable size that are said to have destroyed the Minoan civilization and its primary settlements around the Aegean Sea. The earthquakes and floods caused by the tsunamis were so damaging to the Minoans, many archaeologists agree it that marked the end of the Minoan civilization as it was unable to entirely recover afterwards.

The adverse natural phenomena that followed from this eruption were so notable in the entire region, including Egypt, that many scholars linked them to the biblical events described in the Book of Exodus. In fact, the visible watermarks that were reported by early explorers on the exterior limestone walls of the pyramids, and eventually found in their interior, may be the physical results of the enormous tsunami generated by the eruption of Santorini.

When the Great Pyramid was first opened, it was reported that incrustations of salt deposits, up to one inch thick, were found inside the pyramid. Although, unquestionably, some salt deposits were generated naturally, a chemical analysis revealed that some of the salt from the interior of the pyramid had a mineral content consistent with sea-salt. While this discovery led to many bizarre speculations in the past, when considering the topography of the Nile Delta (a flat terrain barely few feet above sea level), it is easy to see that a great tsunami like that of the 1600 BC, could have easily inundated the entire area, including the Giza Plateau situated at the beginning of the delta.

Once comparing this immense cataclysm to that of Atlantis, many people, and especially those who believe that the Minoan Santorini was Atlantis, are totally convinced that the island's volcanic eruption was the catastrophe Plato was talking about.

> But afterwards there occurred violent earthquakes and floods; and in a single day and night of misfortune all your warlike men in a body sank into the earth, and the island of Atlantis in like manner disappeared in the depths of the sea." [9]

Indeed, without a doubt, the best we had on Plato's Atlantis up until now, was the island of Santorini, the Minoans, and the Santorini eruption of 1600BC. This was never a flawless hypothesis though. Always a big problem with that theory was the fact that Plato's given chronology of 9600 BC had to be discarded. There is another much bigger problem with that theory though. While Santorini itself, undeniably matches the very site where the crown city of Atlantis once stood (talking about the concentric rings of earth and water,) a huge problem with that claim is that Santorini alone never matched Plato's entire description. The primary island of Atlantis, one Plato said was suppose to be nine kilometers away, is missing from the particular setting of 1600 BC. The lack of a perfectly matching site, also allowed for many critics in the past to raise doubts on Santorini, and to continue to question the validity of Plato's story.

So, it goes without saying, this inability to introduce a matching site out of Santorini alone, more often becomes the juncture where many researchers, including supporters of the original Santorini hypothesis, begin to question the validity of the story. So is Atlantis real, or is it a myth?

Contrary to the apparent difficulty in finding Atlantis, it seems that Plato supplied us with enough information to not only locate the lost island but also to recognize it when found. Clearly, we have the chronology of the event and a detailed physical description of the island. We also know of its volcanic composition, and we have all the details of the island's destruction, including a good portrayal of the aftermath. The information provided should be more than sufficient to help identify the island once it is found. Why then is there such great difficulty so far in finding it?

As previously suggested, in addition to other self-imposed difficulties, it seems that the biggest problem in locating Atlantis, by far, is that most people have been looking for it in the wrong time period. As it seems, the only way to have found the primary island was to look for it in the right *chronology* rather than just in the right *topography*, as many people tend to do once they read the story. For example, while Plato made it clear that the story of Atlantis took place around 9600 BC, mainstream scientific conclusions and early story interpretations lead many people to look for Atlantis during the time period of 1600 BC and around the time when the Santorini volcano erupted.

This group of people ultimately realize that other than the island itself and the volcanic eruption that destroyed it—which are both convincing matches—nothing else seems to correspond to Plato's description. So, as they arrive at a dead end, they either give up their search or continue to look for Atlantis elsewhere, and sometimes in the most unusual places.

Of course, there are those that put aside Plato's testimony altogether and, from the very beginning, follow their own presumptions of what Atlantis once was. Often enough, these people not only are looking for Atlantis in the wrong time and continent, but most frequently, they are looking for an ultra-modern civilization that never existed.

Alternatively, though, when one sets aside all personal interpretations and faithfully searches for Atlantis in the right time period (10,000 to 12,000 years ago), then as if by miracle all the previously loose pieces of this great puzzle begin to fit.

First and foremost, the island of Atlantis, an island nearly the size of Crete, emerges out of the sea just a few kilometers north of Santorini. This obviously happens by lowering the Mediterranean Sea by 400 feet, in order to correspond to the sea level during the tenth millennium BC, when Plato said the story of Atlantis took place.

Once the sea is lowered, the Mediterranean looks like a whole different world. Many coastlines drastically change, and Greece as well as the island region around the Aegean Sea becomes nearly unrecognizable as several islands now merge, including the Cyclades Islands which they were connected by a flat terrain, today called the Cyclades Plateau. This now-submerged plateau formed the body of a large island, while the modern islands of Cyclades fashioned rows of mountains that emerged in all the right places. When comparing the submerged prehistoric island of the Cyclades Plateau to Plato's Atlantis, it becomes clear that this must have been the place Plato was talking about. When still above water, the northern portion of this island was entirely comprised of mountains. There was an oblong valley directly below this mountainous region (roughly 555 sq. km) and a second valley closer to the center of the island (roughly 370 sq. km) that was encircled by low-rise mountains. Moreover, and just as Plato depicted, this central valley was two-thirds the size of the oblong valley. Not only does the primary island perfectly match Plato's physical description, but Santorini itself, a setting of an island within an island, falls exactly nine kilometers away from the main island and just as Plato asserted.

Is there any possibility, though, that the matching site at hand may not be Plato's Atlantis? Actually, when considering that no one in the past was able to introduce a perfectly matching site, when comparing those odds against winning the lottery, it appears that finding and identifying Atlantis was always more difficult. Consequently, to dismiss a perfectly matching site it may be as difficult as dismissing the lottery's six winning numbers. In the case of the Cyclades Plateau, as in the case of the lottery example, not only all the physical characteristics flawlessly match Plato's given description, but all the required elements are found to be in the right sequence and exact dimension. We finally have a place where every physical aspect of a topography, the chronology, the volcanic geology, the flora and fauna in that period (including the elephants), the island's destruction by a "great flood", archaeological remnants of an unknown Neolithic civilization in the immediate area, and most importantly DNA evidence (see haplogroup X), all point to a perfect match and a genuine find. The only evidence truly missing from this setting is a 10,000-year-old artifact, although finding one may be more difficult than it sounds.

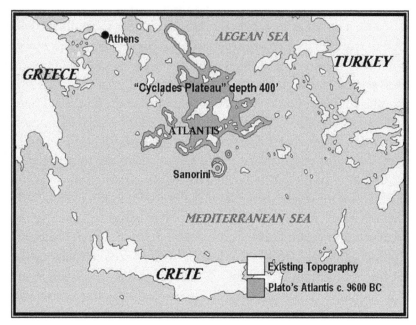

*The island of Atlantis as described by Plato is revealed once the Mediterranean Sea level is lowered by 400feet.*

An island comprising mostly of mountains in the northern portions and along the shore, and encompassing a great plain of an oblong shape in the south extending in one direction three thousand stadia (about 555 square kilometers; 345 square miles), but across the center island it was two thousand stadia (about 370 square kilometers; 230 square miles). Fifty stadia (9km; 6 miles) from the coast was a mountain that was low on all sides...broke it off all round about... the central island itself was five stades in diameter (about 0.92 km; 0.57 miles). [10]

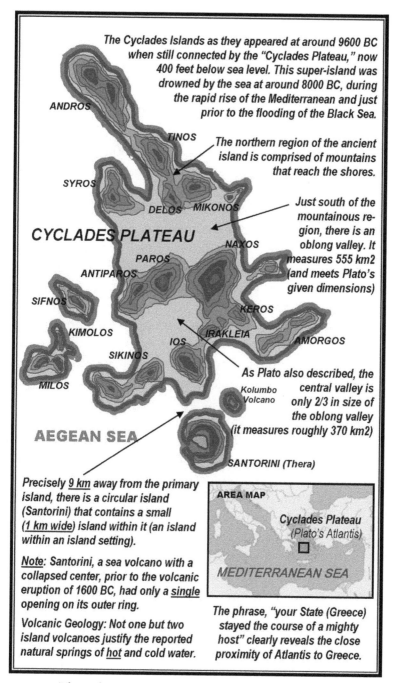

The Cyclades Islands as they appeared at around 9600 BC when still connected by the "Cyclades Plateau," now 400 feet below sea level. This super-island was drowned by the sea at around 8000 BC, during the rapid rise of the Mediterranean and just prior to the flooding of the Black Sea.

The northern region of the ancient island is comprised of mountains that reach the shores.

Just south of the mountainous region, there is an oblong valley. It measures 555 km2 (and meets Plato's given dimensions)

As Plato also described, the central valley is only 2/3 in size of the oblong valley (it measures roughly 370 km2)

Precisely 9 km away from the primary island, there is a circular island (Santorini) that contains a small (1 km wide) island within it (an island within an island setting).

Note: Santorini, a sea volcano with a collapsed center, prior to the volcanic eruption of 1600 BC, had only a single opening on its outer ring.

Volcanic Geology: Not one but two island volcanoes justify the reported natural springs of hot and cold water.

AREA MAP

Cyclades Plateau (Plato's Atlantis) □

MEDITERRANEAN SEA

The phrase, "your State (Greece) stayed the course of a mighty host" clearly reveals the close proximity of Atlantis to Greece.

*The prehistoric super-island of the "Cyclades Plateau" (circa 9600 BC) perfectly matches to Plato's Atlantis.*

While the Cyclades islands are undeniably some of the most beautiful in the world, we must not forget that in the last 10,000 years, this region was carved into existence by one type of natural catastrophe after another. Horrendous earthquakes, unimaginable floods, tsunamis, and frequent volcanic eruptions all contributed to Atlantis's demise and to the formation of these islands. If Atlantian artifacts are not covered beneath several meters of soil or lying below 400 feet of water, they could have been blown to pieces during the 1600 BC volcanic eruption of Santorini or during one of several other volcanic eruptions that occurred over the millennia. Dozens more, less powerful eruptions over the centuries, followed by large tsunamis, also took a toll on the surrounding islands. And, if these conditions were not bad enough, a second volcano in the vicinity periodically caused its own set of disasters.

Although most people don't know this, there is another active volcano eight kilometers northeast of Santorini, with its top sitting just 60 feet beneath the waves. It is known as the Kolumbo Volcano, or *Koloumbos* in Greek. The last known eruption of Kolumbo occurred in 1650 AD, and it was a very violent event as it ejected pumice and ash as far as Turkey and produced pyroclastic flows that killed many people on Santorini at the time. A large tsunami generated by the collapse of the volcano's cone also flooded several islands and caused severe damage up to 150 kilometers away.

Despite the apparent difficulties, though, we must remain hopeful. When looking for archaeological evidence, sometimes with a little luck, anything is possible. Consider the 4,000-year-old city of Akrotiri that survived the unimaginable. Continuous excavations on Santorini and the surrounding islands, as well as at the bottom of the sea between the Cyclades islands, may eventually reveal artifacts or ruins that will finally confirm a 10,000 year old civilization in the area.

Skeptics, though, are never convinced. In fact, they argue that according to the story, Atlantis was swallowed by the sea and vanished, while obviously in this particular case remnants of the island, along with Santorini, were left behind. Also, if not the Santorini eruption of 1600 BC that seems to perfectly match Atlantis' demise, what other natural catastrophe after 9600 BC, they ask, could come close to Plato's description of the end?

While moving forward, first and foremost, we must realize that Plato never mentioned Atlantis's exact end date. The 9600 BC time-frame initially given was the time that the story unfolded, and it did not necessarily reflect the time when Atlantis was lost, as many automatically assume. In fact, Plato pointed out that the end of Atlantis came at a "later time" and after a series of prolonged "portentous earth-quakes and floods."

> But at a later time there occurred portentous earth quakes and floods, and one grievous day and night... And the island of Atlantis in like manner was swallowed up by the sea and vanished. [11]

The mere mention of earthquakes and floods by Plato in the plural form not only confirms that the island's destruction was more gradual, but this statement further corroborates that the periodic floods were most likely associated with the rise of the oceans as earlier indicated. Furthermore, the remark "one grievous day and night", more of a stock phrase, does not necessarily imply that the island was lost within 24 hours, but that the end event occurred at some unknown point in time.

When following Plato's description of the end, it reads, as if for a period of several decades, strong earthquakes and frequent floods (associated with the rise of the oceans) began to take a toll on the island. At some unknown point in time, prior to 8000 BC and just before the flooding of the Black Sea, when the melting of the glaciers reached a climax and the ocean levels began to rise more aggressively, the sea level in the Mediterranean abruptly rose high enough to flood the valleys and lower elevations of Atlantis. This was the particular flood that essentially claimed the island. Practically overnight, the entire island became "impassable and impenetrable," and as Plato explained, "this was caused by the subsidence of the island." Of course, knowing nothing of the natural forces at play, Plato totally misinterpreted the rise of the sea and called it the "gradual sinking" of the island.

> Wherefore also the ocean at that spot has now become impassable and unsearchable, being blocked up by

the shoal of mud which the island created as it settled down. [12]

The conditions during this intense flood must have been horrific as they presumably resembled those of New Orleans in 2005—or worse, those of the tsunami in Thailand in 2004 or Japan in 2011. This particular flood was so formidable that overnight it turned the whole island into a muddy sandbar, or as Plato best explained, into a "shoal of mud." One significant difference between the flood of Atlantis and those other natural disasters is that the flood waters never receded from Atlantis. As the waters continued to rise, the island was forever surrendered to the sea.

This Great Flood and the devastation it brought to the island was what Plato was talking about. Not speaking in literal terms but poetically, Plato said the island on that very day was "swallowed" (claimed) by the sea, and it "vanished." In another paragraph altogether, though, he further describes the particular region and explains that once the flood cycle finally ended, the tops of the surrounding mountains remained above water and formed small islands. Poetically once again, he compared these remaining islets to the "bones of the wasted body" of the "country" that once was there.

> The consequence is, that in comparison of what then was, there are remaining in small islets only the bones of the wasted body, as they may be called, all the richer and softer parts of the soil having fallen away, and the mere skeleton of the country being left. [13]

His description did not end there, though. He went even further and dramatically described the environmental transformation that occurred in the area between 9000 BC and his own time—nearly seven millennia later. He explained that the heavily forested mountains which once supplied timber of sufficient size to cover even the largest houses, now as small islets, could barely provide "sustenance to bees." This is another vital piece of information where Plato perfectly depicts the total transformation of the region and explains how the once large, green islands of the Aegean, from ten millennia ago, ultimately became the small, dry islands we know today.

> But in former days, and in the primitive state of the country, what are now mountains were regarded as hills; and the plains are they are now termed, of Phelleus were full of rich earth, and there was abundance of wood in the mountains. Of this last the traces still remain, for there are some of the mountains which now only afford sustenance to bees, whereas not long ago there were still remaining roofs cut from the trees growing there, which were of a size sufficient to cover the largest houses; and there were many other high trees, bearing fruit, and abundance of food for cattle. [14]

There is little doubt that the particular flood, which destroyed Atlantis and every coastal civilization around the planet simultaneously, is the event that forever after would be referred to as the Great Flood. Atlantis and other civilizations around the world, like the submerged city off the coast of West India, all fell victim to the rising oceans. For the next 1,000 years, as the waters relentlessly continued to claim more and more dry land, all efforts to reignite any of these civilizations apparently failed. This was a chaotic period where people remained scattered, and history obviously ceased to exist.

In a recent scientific text book on marine environments, titled *"Coastal and Marine Geospatial Technologies,"* K. Gaki-Papanastasiou said not only that the ancient Cycladic Island could be the location where Atlantis once stood, but she further agreed that if Atlantis did exist, it was lost due to the rapidly rising sea waters.

> "It is very possible that the famous ancient Atlantis was one of the flourishing city states on the large Cycladic Island (5,282 km$^2$) that was drowned following the rapid sea level rise between 18,000 and 7,000 years ago…. The disappearance of Atlantis may not be owed to tectonic reasons (sudden submergence) but to eustatic ones (marine transgression). If we postulate

that Atlantis was a city-state flourishing around 10,000
- 9,000 years Before Present, that it was located in the
central Aegean Sea, and that the "old" Cycladic Island
was diminishing quickly due to the rapid sea level rise,
it becomes obvious that many coastal Neolithic settlements were drowned by the sea." [15]

Close to 5000 BC (once the oceans and climate stabilized enough),
we begin to see signs of human activity, and a several centuries later,
at around 4000 BC, we see an explosion of human civilizations which
"mysteriously" seem to appear out of nowhere. The Sumerians emerged
in Mesopotamia, the Harappa civilization developed in India and in no
time the "Minoans" began to dominate over the entire Mediterranean.
Practically overnight, these civilizations became masters of architecture, astronomy and possessed incredible skills that neither historians
nor anthropologists can quite explain.

Unfortunately, though, due to the lack of tangible evidence, it
seems that early archaeologists failed to make the connection and to
recognize that many of these cultures were around thousands of years
earlier. In essence, we failed to realize that the incredible megalithic
structures and technological achievements of the fifth and fourth
millennia BC were essentially part of an earlier "renaissance era" that
immediately resumed once the rise of the oceans ended. So when for
the first time a post-Atlantian civilization was detected on Crete, due
to the lack of clear identity, early archaeologists mistakenly renamed
them Minoans after the mythical king of Crete, Minos.

While to this day it is not clear what Minoans called themselves,
it appears that other ancient civilizations, especially the Egyptians,
knew of their close relation to Atlantis. This revelation becomes more
evident with their assertion to Solon that Atlantis was an old adversary of Greece. Strangely, by the time this information was revealed
to Solon, Atlantis was already "lost in history." In fact, the post-Atlantian civilization of the Minoans also ended 800 years prior to that
revelation. Although the Egyptians were fully aware that the Greeks
were not around early enough to have met the Atlantians, they still
named the Atlantians an adversary of Athens. Why would they say
that? Was that a mistake? On the other hand, the Egyptians knew that

before their demise the Minoans and the Athenians were real enemies. Did the Egyptians make a mistake about who was who, or since they knew the Minoans and Atlantians were one and the same, did they take their own knowledge for granted, thinking further clarification was not necessary?

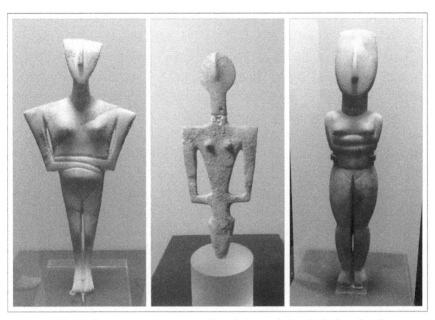

*The prehistoric artifacts were found around the Cyclades islands and predate both the Greek and Minoan civilizations by few thousand years. Most likely they were created by remnants of the same people who escaped the inundation of the Cyclades Plateau, and ultimately reorganized around the smaller islands (then mountaintops of the original landmass).*

Then again, there is also a strong possibility that Plato could have inflated the original Egyptian testimony. While he claimed that the story of Atlantis was entirely true, he may have done what Homer did with Troy, few hundred years earlier. We all know that Homer's Iliad was an entirely fictional story that revolved around a real setting and a historical incident that took place 600 years before Homer himself. In other words, Plato could have created a fable around a real setting and a prehistoric civilization known to ancient Greeks, in which, in order to successfully communicate some of his philosophical views, (divine vs. human, ideal societies vs. corrupt) he filled with familiar matter and details from his own time. Could his ideological story otherwise appeal to his audience if they could not connect or relay to it? Consequently, as in the case of Troy, the true-part of this story should not rest in the story details, but in the physical detection and authentication of Plato's "lost island."

After the eruption of Santorini, the Minoans lasted for another half century or so. By then, the effects of that disaster brought them to their knees and made them easy prey for the mainland Greeks, who finally invaded Crete and helped put an end to the Minoan era. The volcanic eruption of Santorini and the mega tsunamis that followed marked the beginning of the end for this post-Atlantian civilization. With their coastal cities and villages on Crete and those on the surrounding islands destroyed, and without a navy to rely on for protection, many Minoans moved east and settled on the island of Cyprus. Eventually, they moved further east and settled on the shores of the Mediterranean between Syria and Israel. According to historical accounts, though, it seems that the mighty Minoans did not "go quietly into the night." While considering that at that point in time they were, in effect, a "dead" civilization, their influence in the area was enormous—to say the least.

Cypro-Minoan scripts found in Cyprus and around the Middle East proved that the Linear A writing system, developed after the Minoan arrival on the island, had several shared characteristics with the Minoan Linear B system widely used on the island of Crete. Oddly enough, after studying the new Cypro-Minoan writing system and those who used it, mainstream historians decided to call these people Philistines. They furthermore credited the Linear A system to the mysterious and previously unknown Philistines, a literate culture of "sea people" that we are told originated from a region within the Aegean Sea and ultimately migrated to the eastern shores of the Mediterranean around 1200 BC.

There should be no mystery in this case, though. Clearly these mysterious "sea people" were primarily Minoan refugees mixed with other Aegean people who were uprooted not only by the volcanic eruption of Santorini itself but ultimately by the aftermath of that horrible and long-lasting disaster. Without taking into consideration what type of adverse conditions followed this particular volcanic eruption, or how many years its effects lasted, a blast of that magnitude must have severely devastated the entire Aegean region and forced the inhabitants of that area to flee. If not right away, they certainly fled in the years that followed.

Of course there is another strong possibility though that the eruption of Santorini was not just an isolated incident during the end of the Bronze Age. It is highly speculated that the movement of the same tectonic plates, which may have caused the earthquakes in the area and ultimately the eruption of Santorini, could have continued to produce a series of strong earthquakes in that region for another couple of centuries.

A recent study posted in *Stanford News Service* in 1997 titled "Don't Blame the Trojan Horse: Earthquakes Toppled Ancient Cities, Stanford Geophysicist Says," revealed that it is very possible for large earthquakes to be temporarily clustered. The study explained that when a tectonic plate ruptures in one place, it strains another part of the plate boundary and ultimately may cause its collapse after a short time. Until the entire plate boundary ruptures, a cascade of earthquakes can be produced. The period of intense activity can be separated by long time periods when the entire plate strains but does not quite give. In that case, as the strain builds up, the earthquake cycle begins once again.

It is believed that fifty or more cities around the Eastern Mediterranean, between Greece and Israel, fell victim to prolonged earthquakes at the end of the Bronze Age, and more specifically, just prior to 1200 BC when the "sea people" first appeared. If so, it is not hard to envision that the societies affected, given their limited technology, immediately fell apart, thus creating a wave of refugees that traveled the region—either by land or water—and raided all other cities found intact for their own survival. As the region in the Mediterranean that was primarily affected (either by the Santorini eruption or by the earthquakes that followed) was a Minoan territory, most of these refugees must have been of Minoan ancestry. Archaeological evidence pointed out that the residents of Santorini, along with their entire fleet, escaped the volcanic eruption. If so, where did they settle afterwards? Crete, their primary colony, was also devastated by the huge tsunamis that followed. Is it possible that the Minoan refugees were immediately welcomed by another society in the area, or could they have turned into a culture of "sea people" who initially survived by preying on the entire region and on the wealth of others?

According to history, these Minoan refugees (or sea people, if you prefer) eventually settled along the shores of the Middle East. Excavations at Ashkelon in Israel, a known Philistine city, proved that the writing inscribed on several clay pots was actually Cypro-Minoan. While most likely many of these pieces were imported from Cyprus or Crete by early settlers, a particular jar of local clay proved to be the work of a native post-Minoan culture there. There is more evidence, though, to prove that the so-called sea people (or Philistines) were of a Minoan ancestry. The ancient city of Gaza, yet another popular Philistine city, was originally called Minoah, a name clearly founded by Cretans.

The influence of the Minoans on the island of Cyprus was also quite significant. For starters, the language transformation on the island to Linear A was so widespread that led some historians to theorize that the enigmatic Philistines may have originated there. Despite the scientific confusion though, is worth to mention that Cyprus is the only country in the world which still annually holds a week-long celebration in remembrance of the Great Flood. Although this popular festival is linked by its Christian population to the biblical flood, is it also possible that it essentially commemorates an event that over the millennia was kept alive by the so-called sea people or better yet, the post-Atlantian Minoans?

To better understand how the climatic and ecological changes (and ultimately the rise of the sea) affected coastal civilizations in the Mediterranean, one must follow the work of Dr. Francois Doumenge (director of the Oceanographic Institute of Monaco and Secretary General of the International Commission for the Scientific Exploration of the Mediterranean Sea, Monaco).

In 1996, Dr. Doumenge gave a presentation at the United Nations University Headquarters. Although his presentation had nothing to do with archaeology or anthropology directly, Dr. Doumenge presented a long-term historical look of the Mediterranean and the series of environmental crises that had affected it over the millennia. To a certain extent, he confirmed past theories that during the Messinian period the Strait of Gibraltar had remained closed for a period of 100,000 to 200,000 years, during which time the Mediterranean had completely evaporated. This, he explained, happened several times between five and six million years ago. As a consequence, the dry basin of the Mediterranean retained giant salt deposits with a total volume exceeding 1.5 million square kilometers. The total water evaporation between five and six million years ago, as well as its continuous evaporation and refill of seawater either from the Atlantic or Red Sea, also explains the higher salinity currently found in the Mediterranean.

Dr. Doumenge also further revealed that the Mediterranean went through another crisis during the last ice age beginning 18,000 years ago. He explained that not only had the last ice age caused severe effects on the Mediterranean's ecosystem, but the 500-foot lower sea level had exposed hundreds of thousands of square miles of land.

The Adriatic Sea was mostly dry land; the Aegean Sea was about 40 percent smaller; and the enlarged Sicilian and African coast, at modern-day Tunisia, nearly merged. The much smaller Black Sea, a freshwater lake at that time, was heavily draining into the Mediterranean with its water flowing southward along the coast of modern-day Turkey all the way to the northern coast of Africa.

The combined effects during the last ice age were so profound that the Mediterranean Basin was divided into three separate ecosystems. The far eastern portion of the Mediterranean, which was essentially cut off by the stream of freshwater that flowed down from the Black Sea, remained warmer, and the region around Egypt and Cyprus was more like a semitropical setting. This early semitropical climate in the prehistoric Middle East also explains the existence of the Fertile Crescent, a fertile territory that extended from the Nile valley, it followed the coast of the Eastern Mediterranean to southeastern Turkey, then turned southwards toward the Mesopotamia region and the shores of the Persian Gulf. This area, which ultimately became the cradle of civilization as we know it, was also the home of eight Neolithic originator crops important to early agriculture, and the home of four of the five most important species of domesticated animals (cows, goats, pigs, and sheep).

The Central Mediterranean, in contrast, maintained its present temperature and characteristics. The Western Basin, connected and continuously refilled via the Strait of Gibraltar, retained much colder temperatures similar to those of the North Sea. This also explains the large population of Blue Whales in the western part of the Mediterranean, still present to this day.

While reviewing Dr. Doumenge's study from 1996, as well as the latest study in *Science News* in 2010, we realize that the planet went through a massive cataclysm that started around 13000 BC, intensified between 9000 BC and 8000 BC, and finally began to stabilize between 7000 BC and 6000 BC. During this period, not only did the seas rise by 400 feet or more, but the rising waters seem to have literally swallowed all physical evidence that could suggest the existence of another advanced civilization during our prehistory.

Is it possible, however, that all traces of prehistoric civilizations are completely lost? Although archaeological sites like that of Gobekli Tepe help validate their existence, unfortunately, the burden of proof rests with sunken cities, like those off the west coast of India and that of Atlantis. Should we assume then that the evidence of all past civilizations lay at the bottom of the sea, or is it possible somehow that more artifacts in higher elevations may have survived and await our discovery?

Fortunately, as it seems, science never ceases to surprise us. On October 23, 1991, an incredible article in the *Los Angeles Times* caught many people's attention. The article was titled "Sphinx's New Riddle—Is It Older Than Experts Say? Archeologists, Geologists Cite Study of Weathering Patterns, but Egyptologists Say Findings Can't Be Right."

As the title of the article insinuates, after extensive geological research on the Giza Plateau and the Great Sphinx at that time, the evidence pointed to the possibility that the Sphinx may be at least twice as old as the pyramids and could conservatively date as far back as 7000 BC.

As expected, such an announcement caused a firestorm of controversy and a fierce argument among mainstream archaeologists since such a conclusion contradicted everything the mainstream academia "knew" about ancient Egypt.

When geologists presented their results at the Geological Society of America, they mentioned that the weather patterns on the monument convinced them that they were from another period much older than previously estimated. Until then, Egyptologists and mainstream archaeologists thought the Sphinx was built by the Pharaoh Khafre around 2500 BC. The evidence collected, though, after a series of unprecedented studies at the Giza site, suggested that the monument had already been there for thousands of years before Khafre.

More specifically, the research team noticed that the Sphinx was actually carved into a limestone bedrock and essentially sits inside a ditch. The walls of this ditch offered the researchers the first tantalizing clues. They were heavily weathered by water, suggesting that the ditch was dug much earlier than 3000 BC, when rainfall in the area was much heavier than it has been in the last few thousand years. Of course, as mentioned earlier, according to Dr. Doumenge the last time rainfall in this area was heavy would have been around 8,000 BC, during the rise of the Mediterranean and prior to the flooding of the Black Sea.

Joining geologist Robert M. Schoch of Boston University in the research were Thomas L. Dobecki, a Houston geophysicist, and John Anthony West, an Egyptologist of New York.

The team of scientists showed that the limestone bed surrounding the monument, part of which was exposed when the Sphinx was first carved, has weathered far longer than had been previously thought. In addition, significant erosion differences between the Sphinx and other structures of unmistakable origin further indicated that the Sphinx was a much-older structure.

The scientific team also conducted the first seismic tests ever allowed at the site, which essentially reveal the age of a structure by measuring how sound waves move through rock. As weathering creates pores in rocks, the speed at which the waves travel can tell scientists about the porosity of the rock, and the sound waves can measure how much of a structure has weathered. In turn, that tells them how long it has been exposed to the elements.

Needless to say, and as expected, Egyptologists continue to maintain that the Great Sphinx must have been the creation of Khafre, not only because it is contained within the same tomb complex, but also as they indicate, the face of the Sphinx also resembles Khafre. Interestingly though, the same type tests on the face of the Sphinx indicated that the head is as old as its body, thus making it much older than the rest of the monuments. Ultimately, Mr. Schoch and his team concluded that when Khafre began construction on this site, not only could he have refurbished the monument, but he also could have altered the face.

If Mr. Schoch and his team are correct in their assessment, a few questions still remain to be answered. Who constructed the Great Sphinx nearly 10,000 years ago, and why? Is it possible that the rise of the Egyptian civilization around the 3rd millennium BC was not a new development, but a legacy that continued over a much older civilization in the area? Even more importantly, does the conclusion of another prehistoric civilization erecting this great structure further validate all other rumors surrounding this monument?

More specifically, in the past it has been claimed repeatedly that there are cavities under the Sphinx, including one that holds the Hall of Records. For those not familiar with this story, the Hall of Records is believed to be a small chamber beneath the Sphinx that housed the history of Atlantis in papyrus scrolls. It is also how, reportedly, the Egyptian priests initially became aware of the lost civilization.

Surprisingly enough, the belief that there are cavities below the monument, as well as a tomb belonging to King Harmais, is not a recent claim. This was first suggested by Pliny the Elder (23 AD - 79 AD), a renowned Roman author and military commander.

While modern-day archaeologists categorically deny the existence of such a chamber, interestingly enough, ground-penetrating radar implies that indeed there are unexplained cavities below this monument. If so, was Pliny the Elder correct? Is it possible to accept, as other researchers previously asserted, that around 10500 BC, Atlantians sealed the hall away with scrolls of their accumulated knowledge, just as the Hebrews did with the Dead Sea Scrolls 8,000 years later?

Many mainstream Egyptologists disagree. In fact, not only do they deny such claims, but surprisingly, they also dismiss Mr. Schoch's research. According to them, "the people of that region would not have had the technology, the governing institutions, or even the will to build such a structure thousands of years before Khafre's reign." Why do they dismiss the scientific research of Mr. Schoch and insist on their previous conclusions? Clearly, the assessment that the Great Sphinx is a much-older structure was not reached without the scientific data to support it. So selectively ignoring other scientific data and the notion of "what we don't know or don't understand simply does not exist" is far from scientific. Taking such a position against the scientific evidence, not to mention ancient testimony, nearly takes us back to a time when we insisted that the Earth was flat.

Incidentally, though, just when more critics started to remind us that no one so early in time could have constructed the monument of the Sphinx, to everyone's amazement, another remarkable discovery in the Mediterranean region proved once again that our ancestors 12,000 years ago were more advanced and capable than we are willing to give them credit for. Without a doubt, this latest finding not only reinforces Mr. Schoch's claim that the Sphinx could have been created 10,000 years ago, but it further confirms Plato's testimony of another advanced civilization in the area during our prehistory.

On February 19, 2010, *Newsweek* published an article titled "History in the Remaking: A Temple Complex in Turkey that Predates Even the Pyramids Is Rewriting the Human Evolution."

The site of Gobekli Tepe, currently the world's oldest archaeological site, is estimated to have been erected 12,000 years ago, if not earlier. It is a massive site that features 20 large, round structures, each up to 30 meters (100 feet) in diameter. Each round structure features huge, T-shaped pillars (some up to 6.9 meters in height), which at one point held a roof system overhead. Carvings of animals on these T-shaped pillars include foxes, lions, hyenas, cranes, ducks, scorpions, and snakes—among others.

Although not a great deal is known of this incredible archaeological site that predates the pyramids by at least 7,000 years, Gobekli Tepe further validates previous claims that prehistoric humans were more organized and advanced than historians and anthropologists were previously willing to accept.

Of course, contrary to the mounting evidence which points towards such conclusion, some skeptics still argue that Gobekli Tepe refutes the idea of an organized society at the time, for its structures, according to them, were constructed without the infrastructure of a known civilization. Is it possible, then, that two dozen or more monumental assemblies on this site that imply certain complexity and organization that rivals those of ancient Sumer, were constructed by a horde of hunters and gatherers on their spare time, or does Gobekli Tepe itself makes the case for such early human organization?

We must also not ignore the possibility that this mega site, although initially labeled by its founders as a place of worship, could have been an early human settlement instead. Evidence of daily activities, such as flint knapping and food preparation, suggests that Gobekli Tepe could have been, at least partially, a residential site with a large population. In a study published in *Current Anthropology* in 2011, archaeologist Ted Banning of the University of Toronto argued that some of the large buildings, especially those with the decorative pillars, could have been large communal houses "similar in some ways to the large plank houses of the Northwest Coast of North America with their impressive house posts and totem poles." If so, Banning said, "they would likely have housed quite large households, an extremely early example of what the French anthropologist, Claude Lévi-Strauss, called 'house societies'. Such societies often use house structures for competitive display, locations for rituals, and explicit symbols of social units."

Additional prehistoric settlements in the region carrying round structures as well, like that of Khirokitia in Cyprus or the city of Jericho in Palestine, not only suggest that Gobekli tepe could have been occupied by its builders, but this mega-site reinforces the suggestion of an advanced prehistoric civilization in the area.

Is it possible that Gobekli Tepe, and the monument of the Great Sphinx, could be remnants of the same advanced civilization Plato was talking about, one that aggressively was advancing eastwards against its neighbors? If so, is it also possible to further assume that the oppressed, at first opportunity, buried the outpost of Gobekli Tepe thus eliminating the possibility for the trespassers ever reestablishing control over that area? According to the chief archaeologist at Gobekli Tepe, Klaus Schmidt, the site not only was abandoned abruptly around 8000 BC, but it was deliberately buried all at once! This is how archaeologists explain most of the structures on this site remained intact.

What happened to the oppressors, though? Where did they go once they lost control of the region? Just like the post-Atlantian Minoans, after the volcanic eruption of Santorini they scattered eastwards around the shores of the Middle East, is it possible that the last Great Flood forced remnants of that once advanced culture deeper into the Fertile Crescent, towards the Mesopotamian region, where they ultimately helped the local population establish yet another great civilization, like that of ancient Sumer? Is it possible that refugees of this Mediterranean culture, which slowly dissented upon the Mesopotamian region between 8000 and 7000 BC, not only brought with them the story of the "Great Flood", but along with it, some of their technological skills, including agriculture and astronomy? If not, who then were the mysterious Proto-Euphratean people, as archaeologists call them today, who descended to Mesopotamia from a region unknown and laid the foundation for the Sumerian civilization to build upon?

While, more and more evidence points to the possibility that "Plato's Atlantians" may ultimately be the missing link to help answer many of these questions, we must not ignore that more archaeological finds from within the Mediterranean region raise the possibility of even more unknown civilizations. One such artifact that puzzled archaeologists and historians for more than a century is the Phaistos Disk.

The Phaistos Disc, first discovered by Luigi Pernier in 1908, was named after the location where it was found in the Palace of Phaistos on the island of Crete. Although its age cannot yet be conclusively verified, some archaeologists estimate that it could be roughly 4,000 years old. Is it possible that it could be an older artifact? It is certainly a possibility. The problem, in identifying this object, is that the inscription on the disc does not belong to any known language in our recorded history. No matter how far back we go, we cannot find anything else similar in order to be able to decipher its message.

The disc is roughly 15 centimeters in diameter (almost 6 inches) and is covered on both sides with a spiral of stamped symbols. A total of 247 symbols on both sides of the disc comprise 45 signs that could translate to either words or numbers. While the disc's purpose, meaning, and/or geographical origin so far remain unsolved, it makes it one of the most famous mysteries of archaeology.

If the disc—as some archaeologists speculate—was created during the Minoan period, why do the symbols on it not match anything else from that period? Furthermore, why would a disc with strange symbols that were meaningless to its caretakers be carefully stored under the palace of Phaistos and, out of all places, in the main cell of an underground temple depository? These basement-type cells were accessible only from above, and they were found to be sealed with a thin layer of plaster. Ironically enough, inside the same cell, and only inches away from the disc, archaeologists uncovered another tablet that had inscribed the language commonly used at the time.

So is the Phaistos Disc a Minoan-made artifact as some archaeologists claim, or is it possible that it belongs to another civilization yet to be found? Or is it perhaps a memento from the Minoans' own past, possibly when they were still known as Atlantians? No one knows.

Of course, it could always be another trophy brought from the New World along with the Mayan headpiece illustrated in the famous Minoan fresco. As the pictograms on the disc slightly resemble those of the Aztecs, is it possible that the Phaistos Disc could be another souvenir brought straight out of the Americas?

# THE HUMAN GENOME

*The Human Genome: A Miracle or Genetics?*
*-- The Panspermia Hypothesis.*
*NASA Confirms Alien Life Is Found on Earth.*

During the early part of the twentieth century, mainstream science theorized that the modern human evolved out of a series of ape mutations that undeniably led to the development of the Neanderthals of whom ultimately the modern human evolved from. No gaps in the theory, no doubts.

Even while not too long ago archaeologists began to unearth more and more evidence of other prehistoric hominids that could have some connection to the origins of modern man, continuous studies still indicates that, at least theoretically, the Neanderthals remain our closest matching cousins. In fact, a detailed analysis shows that while the Neanderthals and modern human lineages maybe separated approximately half a million years ago, we still share more than 99.5 percent of the same DNA.

So assuming this mutation took place half a million years ago, and science estimates that the final version of *Homo sapiens* appeared roughly 200,000 years ago, where is the scientific evidence of evolution to fill in the 300,000 years gap? Most importantly, is it possible for a mutation to take place and within 300,000 years to genetically alter a hominid species into that of a modern man?

According to a recent scientific study, we are told that *Homo sapiens* "suddenly" appeared in South Africa 200,000 years ago, and their exodus from the African continent took place about 100,000 years later. According to the same study, the new species were far more superior to all other species that coexisted during the same period, including the Neanderthals, which surprisingly were still around, competing as a separate species! From there, we all know the end of that story. *Homo sapiens* not only quickly dominated the planet, but also helped partly to exterminate their competition while in constant search for new and better hunting grounds.

What really caused this "sudden" mutation in the human genome though, that not only allowed Homo sapiens to appear nearly overnight, in chronological terms, but also (and most importantly) equipped them with certain superiority over all other hominids?

Although past mainstream scientific studies indicated that it took about a million years of evolution for the Cro-Magnon Man (*Homo erectus*) to evolve into the modern *Homo sapiens*, there is no conclusive evidence to support that theory. And to make matters worse for science, several independent scientific studies not only prove that *Homo sapiens* appeared rather suddenly, but more interestingly, all genes lead back to an original male and a female! This mystery, the mystery of the human transformation, is what many scientists today refer to as the "missing link" in human evolution. And while this mystery persists, many more studies continue to take place.

Among many early scientific theories, another explanation given was that the mutation was caused by infecting bacteria! Bacteria, really! According to this theory, 223 new genes suddenly appeared without their required genomic predecessors. In order for this mutation to take place, it would be extremely difficult, if not impossible.

For starters, humans have relatively sheltered DNA—not to mention that the process for a lateral gene transfer involves a series of complicated measures in order for anything like this to happen. In simple terms, for this mutation to work, a gene must first find its way into the nucleus of the cells that give rise to sperm and egg; otherwise it cannot be passed on. And even in the event that somehow this happens, the transferred gene must be arranged in the perfect format that allows for its long-term maintenance and further reproduction.

Once considering all this, it is not a big surprise that a later analysis proved that the previous study was grossly exaggerated, and suggested that only an insignificant amount of genes can ever be transferred to humans by bacteria enough to cause such mutation. In other words, modern science has not yet conclusively determined where these 223 mystery genes came from, and what, or who, caused the mutation that allowed *Homo sapiens* to suddenly appear in South Africa.

In 1953, two British scientists, Francis Crick and James Watson, unraveled the structure of human DNA, and ten years later, they received the Nobel Price for their discovery. Although Francis Crick was clearly a member of the mainstream scientific community, he believed and supported unconventional theories that were not exactly acceptable by his colleagues. Crick not only enthusiastically supported the Panspermia theory, but twenty or so years later, along with biochemist Leslie Orgel, wrote a paper discussing also the possibility of "directed" Panspermia (the theory that organisms were deliberately transmitted to Earth by intelligent beings from another planet).

*Panspermia*, arriving from a Greek word, literally translates into "seeds (of life) everywhere," it hypothesizes that life (the seed/sperm of life) exists everywhere in the universe and is distributed around by meteorites, comets, asteroids, and planetoids. The theory proposes that microbial life can survive the effects of space as it gets trapped in debris that is ejected into space when planets with life collide with smaller objects. The bacteria can remain dormant for an extended period of time until the debris that contains the bacteria randomly collides once again with another planet. According to the theory, under ideal conditions, the bacteria become active once again and the evolution of life begins. This is not a far-fetched hypothesis considering that interplanetary transfer of material is a well-documented event and is especially evidenced in meteorites of Martian origin.

Most of us remember of the Martian Meteor that in 1996 made headlines around the world. The discovery was first announced with scientists indicating that the contents of the meteor contained fossilized microscopic bacteria. Although quickly afterwards the study was contested, in 2009, another team of scientists, when thoroughly examined the meteorite and discovered that it contained magnetite crystals in it, they reasserted that there was "strong evidence that life may have existed on ancient Mars." By then, it was already too late. The public and media had lost track of this story.

In May of 2001, two researchers from the University of Naples, geologist Bruno D'Argenio and molecular biologist Giuseppe Geraci claimed to have found live extraterrestrial bacteria inside a meteorite. Incredibly enough, their study showed that bacteria were wedged inside the crystal structure of minerals, and they were resurrected when a sample of the rock was placed in a culture medium!

In a book published in 1999 by Kluwer Academic Publishers, named *Enigmatic Microorganisms and Life in Extreme Environments: Cellular Origin and Life in Extreme Habitats,* Russell H. Vreeland and William D. Rosenzweig, biologists at West Chester University in Pennsylvania, reported that while analyzing Salado salt crystals, in hope of finding some biological record of prehistoric microbial life trapped in these crystals, discovered what is believed to be the world's oldest surviving life forms that were able to remain in suspended animation for a period of 250 million years. This incredible discovery, needless to say, gives the Panspermia theory further scientific consideration.

On December 2, 2010, the following amazing announcement dominated for a brief moment the airwaves around the globe: NASA confirms alien life is found on Earth.

This declaration actually ended up reinforcing the theory that not only bacteria can survive in the most harmful environments, but, they can also be resurrected and thrive on a planet that may supports life of different molecular structure. More specifically, in Mono Lake California, scientists have discovered some bacteria that have a significant difference in their molecular structure than all other life forms on Earth. While all life as we know it is made of carbon, hydrogen, oxygen, nitrogen, phosphorus, and sulfur, the newly found bacteria are made from all of the above, except phosphorus. Amazingly enough, in the place of phosphorus, this organism contains arsenic, a lethal poison to all other life forms on the planet. In fact, not only does it breathe arsenic, but it needs arsenic to regenerate.

Although the announcement stopped short of proclaiming that the bacteria may be of extraterrestrial origin, the incredible discovery not only turned our understanding of life upside down, but it further confirmed that life itself can have a different molecular structure, and that knowledge raises the possibility that life can more easily be found in other planets and in environments that previously we thought it was impossible to exist. This discovery clearly proves that it is no longer impossible for life to exist in places like Titan, a moon around Jupiter, that— according to NASA—contains arsenic and therefore, harmful to life as we know it.

Whether life on Earth was due to Panspermia or not, Fred Hoyle, a known English astronomer known for his contribution to the theory of stellar nucleosynthesis and also a strong proponent of Panspermia, in regards to human evolution, once famously stated the following:

> The chance that higher life forms might have emerged
> this way (by evolution) is comparable to the chance that
> a tornado sweeping through a junkyard might assemble
> a Boeing 747 from the materials therein. [16]

Setting aside the various theories on how life on our planet may have started, in regards to human evolution, if nature on its own could not have done the final DNA manipulation for *Homo sapiens* to exist, then who did it? Is it possible that the mysterious 223 DNA genes that ultimately define *Homo sapiens* were literally inserted into place by the anthropomorphic gods of antiquity, who—in essence, and according to ancient Sumerians—combined their DNA or "blood" (for lack of better words) with an existing species from Earth, thus creating the first humans in their own image?

Does this bizarre hypothesis, as unbelievable as it may sound, explain how all humanity can be traced back to an original couple or a small group of "evolved" individuals? Of course it does! Is this a far-fetched hypothesis? Maybe it is, although in that case how do we otherwise explain that every religion on Earth, from the dawn of time insists that humans were manipulated into existence by another "higher power?" And if so, how sure are we that this higher power was actually a spiritual power performing physical acts?

Many of us remember the original Adam story that was widely published in 1997. The study pointed out that when tracing the Y chromosome, which sons only inherit from their fathers, it traces the origin of every man to a single male who lived approximately 200,000 years ago along with the original Eve who was also identified a decade or so earlier! The study went further and pointed out in more detail that, after independent investigations of minute mutations on the Y chromosome, the original Adam and Eve lived in Africa or South Africa, to be more exact. From there, once they overpopulated the African continent, they continued their exodus and ultimately migrated over the entire planet.

Although when reading about this study, many Judean-Christian theologians will rush to point to the Bible's "divine" content that in essence, more or less claims the same, the "truth" may be quite more startling. This scientific discovery, actually, raises several questions that neither science nor Christian scholars may have the answers for.

How can science explain that humankind traces back to an original male and female, or a handful of individuals, unless, of course, they subscribe to the notion of creation? And furthermore, how do they explain that an ancient civilization like the Sumerians had already asserted such information 6,000 years ago, unless they are willing to endorse the Sumerian stories of creation?

Christian scholars also may have a slight difficulty answering some of the questions, as well. For example, how can they explain that the story of Adam and Eve, as many other stories in the Old Testament of the Bible, are literal copies out of the much older Sumerian faith that was taught thousands of years earlier?

So, where did the ancient Sumerians, the oldest known civilization on Earth, obtain their information from? Did they invent the original story of creation and simply got lucky? How could a six-thousand-year-old culture possibly presume that humanity traces back to a small group of people? Most importantly, how did they know that humans emerged out of Africa, unless as they also asserted, the humans were purposely placed in South Africa by the gods shortly after their creation.

# THE SUMERIANS

*What Did Sumerians Know of Intelligent Design? -- Is Planet X Real? -- Were Humans Created by the Gods in Need of Servants? -- Who Operated the Prehistoric Gold Mines of South Africa? -- Is the Old Testament a Copy of a Much-Older Original? -- Does God Need Gold and Other Precious Metals?*

Known as the oldest advanced civilization on Earth, the Sumerians flourished more than 6,000 years ago in southern Mesopotamia (in Greek, it translates as the land "between the rivers"), a territory that is now modern-day Iraq.

This fascinating culture was discovered by British, German, and French archaeologists during the 19th century while excavating in southern Iraq, in a region between the Tigris and Euphrates rivers. Although, almost immediately, there was confusion among them over whether or not the newly found artifacts belonged to the Babylonian culture, a few decades later, it became apparent that the Sumerians, not only preceded the Babylonians by at least 2,000 years but in fact the Babylonians—as other cultures who dominated the same region over the millennia—expanded their own civilization on the Sumerian culture and beliefs.

Once archaeologists sifted through the tens of thousands of artifacts and text clay tablets, the Sumerians were properly credited for developing a distinct writing system (one the Babylonians nearly copied) and for establishing a set of religious beliefs that were adopted by all other civilizations that followed in the Middle East. Most importantly, though, they were credited with many technological achievements that were thousands of years ahead of their time.

Six thousand years ago, they were already operating an elaborate form of government with written laws, and they were practicing complex mathematics and science. In fact, when it came to mathematics and astrology, in a way, they were more advanced than our own civilization of the 19th century! Tablets from this period, among various systems of measurements, include multiplication tables, prime numbers, quadratic formulas, geometry, and trigonometry. They even possessed tables of Pythagorean Triples;" that is, trios of numbers which satisfy the variables A, B, and C in the classic Pythagorean theorem (A squared plus B squared equals C squared).

In physical applications, they had already developed an elaborate system of mass-scale agriculture that heavily relied on irrigation technology and could support city populations of up to a million people.

The most intriguing aspect of this civilization though was their unbelievable knowledge of the stars. The word *unbelievable* actually may be an understatement! Six thousand years ago, they had developed methods to accurately measure the distances between stars, a practice that only recently was reinvented by modern science! Their vast knowledge of the stars also helped them create an annual calendar that had a timeline based upon the zodiac constellations, and it was divided by time periods very similar to ours.

Their knowledge of astronomy, however, did not end with another mundane observation of stars for the sake of time keeping. Surprisingly enough, they knew the precise layout and characteristics of our solar system, as well as the location and trajectories of all the planets, including Pluto, which was not found until 1930! Even more incredibly, they knew the visual color of each planet! They knew Mars was red, while Neptune and Uranus were bluish green, and so on. How is that possible? How could a primitive culture possess such information without modern detection devices? Where did that knowledge come from? Not only did they know about the rings of Saturn, but they also knew of the asteroid belt between Mars and Jupiter, of which they had their own theory for its creation.

They also believed in the existence of another yet to be discovered planet in our solar system. They called this tenth planet Nibiru (it means "the planet of the crossing".) And just as its name insinuates, the Sumerians insist that every 3,600 years, Nibiru—with its very elongated and elliptical trajectory—cuts through the plane of our solar system between Mars and Jupiter, at a 90 degree angle.

According to their detailed descriptions, Nibiru—once a wandering planet—was ultimately caught by the gravity of our newly formed solar system. More than four billion years ago, after all the planets had already formed and positioned in their orbits, planet Earth (referred to by the Sumerians as Tiamat) was a larger watery planet that revolved around the Sun in an orbit farther out in the solar system, between Mars and Jupiter.

During one of the early crossings of Nibiru, four billion years ago, a moon orbiting Nibiru collided with Tiamat and ultimately pushed the fractured planet, with what was left to become its moon, into a new orbit around the Sun. In its brand new orbit, Tiamat became the Earth, and the Moon we know today. The Sumerians further explained that if the debris left behind by the cosmic collision was not absorbed by the exoplanets, it was scattered in the vacuum of space, or became the Asteroid Belt. Eventually, after several more passes and few more adjustments made to the outer planets of our solar system, Nibiru finally established itself in a fixed, elongated orbit around our sun and still continues to cross (or better yet, slice) through our solar system between Mars and Jupiter every 3,600 years.

"A far-fetched hypothesis," some may say. If so, why would the Sumerians invent such an elaborate story six thousand years ago, especially for no particular reason? And if they manufactured this story, from where did they obtain their scientific knowledge, in order to create such a plausible tale to begin with? Moreover, how do we explain the Akkadian, Babylonian, and Egyptian claims describing the same planet slicing through our solar system every so often? Should those testimonies be dismissed as well? Finally, what about the Earth's alleged cosmic collision claim? Can such an event be supported scientifically, and is there another unknown planet in our solar system yet to be discovered?

The Titius-Bode Law, established initially by Johann Daniel Titius in 1766 and followed by Johann Elbert Bode in 1768, was a hypothesis that mathematically rationalized the semi-major axes of the six known planets at the time (Mercury, Venus, Earth, Mars, Jupiter, and Saturn), and further predicted the existence of another planet in the void between Jupiter and Mars. When William Herschel discovered Uranus in 1781 and the planet's orbit matched the law almost perfectly, this led astronomers to the conclusion that there should be another planet between the orbits of Mars and Jupiter. In 1800, while determined to bring the solar system into order, astronomers began an extensive search for the missing planet between Mars and Jupiter. Instead of a large planet though, they found several smaller planetary bodies that although at first they classified as planets, later they demoted those as large asteroids—or dwarf planets. Such was Ceres, the first dwarf planet found in the asteroid belt with a diameter of 950 kilometers. Pallas was the second with a diameter of 530 kilometers. Shortly after, in 1807, two more dwarf planets were found in the region: Juno and Vesta.

Interestingly enough, in 1802, soon after the discovery of Ceres and Pallas, Heinrich Olbers, a German physician and astronomer, suggested that the two planets were fragments of a much-larger planet which once occupied the region and had suffered an internal explosion or destruction by a comet millions of years earlier. Was his hypothesis, which in essence corroborated the Sumerian claim, just an amazing coincidence?

Over time, the Olbers hypothesis fell from favor due to the fact that not only an enormous amount of energy would have been required to obliterate a planet, but the low mass of debris in the asteroid belt did not amount to the mass of an entire planet. Another concern by modern scientists was the difficulty to prove that all the debris in the asteroid belt consists of material from the same planet. Why would anyone, though, expect that all debris in the asteroid belt was generated out of the same planet? When two celestial bodies collide, the immense debris should be of both planets; not to mention that, billions of years later, more foreign debris can settle into the same orbit. So if NASA technically concludes that the isotopic compositions of the objects found in the Asteroid Belt include two primary types of debris, this evidence should be significant enough—not only to support Olbers theory, but also the Sumerian claim. Of course, until the recent NASA mission to Vesta and Ceres returns with such positive results, and/or proves that a planetary collision took place there billions of years ago, we can only speculate such a hypothesis. Still, what is most interesting about this mission is that NASA also believes, just as the Sumerians did, that the space debris in the Asteroid Belt was collected there just "immediately after" the full formation of our solar system, and this was their primary reason to go there and to investigate further. What else could have caused this debris, then? Is it possible that early astronomers gave up on Heinrich Olbers' theory too soon? What if the planet between Mars and Jupiter was not totally destroyed, but rather pushed into a new trajectory?

An interesting part of this mission is that NASA believes that Ceres is a watery planetoid, and they expect to find it either covered in ice, or with large amounts of water trapped beneath its surface! If so, is there a possibility that Ceres, whose spectral characteristics suggest a composition similar to that of a carbonaceous chondrite, was once part of the watery Tiamat? Vesta, on the other hand, a water-poor achondridic asteroid, not only has a completely different composition from Ceres, but is believed to be a planetoid associated with many other smaller objects in the solar system, including most near-Earth asteroids. Is it possible that Vesta, and most V-type near-Earth debris, could be remnants from the colliding planet that ultimately helped push the fractured Tiamat in its new orbit, as the Sumerians suggested? Most importantly, could the prehistoric Earth survive such a collision?

In 2001, after an eight-year extensive study held by Robin Canup of the Southwest Research Institute, she pointed that a planetary collision with Earth not only may have in reality created the Moon, but in fact, may have helped to jumpstart the Earth's rotation! Prior to the completion of her study and that conclusion, Miss Canup extensively worked with William Ward and Alastair Cameron, who represented one of two separate research groups that helped develop the original impact theory during the 1970s.

Unlike earlier studies, though, where researchers thought that the moon was debris left behind from the colliding planet, today—as scientists discovered that the isotopic compositions of the Earth and the Moon are nearly identical—they have concluded that the Moon was, in fact, a piece off the Earth and not debris from the colliding planet.

The primary objective of the new study was not only to demonstrate that a collision had taken place, but also to better explain how—in the aftermath—both bodies ended up in their present geological condition. For example, scientists already know that in contrast with Earth, which is loaded with iron (especially deep in its core), the Moon contains very little iron. This fundamental difference between the two objects led scientists to conclude that if the Moon was created from a past cosmic collision, it was pieced together out of the Earth's crust, which contains much less iron.

Of course, the latest hypothesis contradicted an earlier theory where the Earth and Moon were pieced together after the Earth was completely demolished in a planetary crash. The new research focused on a lighter impact. Backed by several computer simulations, the study established that about four billion years ago, and shortly after the creation of the solar system, the Earth collided with another unknown planetary object in our solar system which, as previously suggested, revolved around the Sun. The scientists further concluded that the trajectory of this unknown planet caused it to cross with Earth's orbit on a regular basis. Ultimately, the two planets collided; and from this collision, the Moon was born! According to this study though, the impact was more of a glancing blow from the rear and at an angle, rather than a head-on collision. As for the debris, if it did not get reabsorbed to create the Moon, it was expanded in space or fell back to Earth.

According to several computer simulations, this scenario could primarily take place if two conditions were met: a) the collision was more of a glancing blow from behind and not a head-on collision and b) the Earth must have been fully established by the time of the collision; otherwise, it could have never recovered. The same study also projected that this impact could have been what started or modified the Earth's rotation!

Although the particular study did not go as far as to examine the possibility of whether Earth, at one point, could have revolved around the Sun between Mars and Jupiter, it otherwise validates every other aspect from the Sumerian claim. So is it possible that the Sumerians were right all along?

When comparing the information included in this study and the strikingly similar story provided by the Sumerians, one must ask: How could an ancient civilization concoct such a hypothesis, and for what reason? In a stable galactic neighborhood, six millennia ago, what possible motive could the Sumerians have to invent such a fantastic story? Or is it possible, as they claim, they were merely repeating information given to them by their gods? If so, who were these creatures that shared planetary collision stories with the Sumerians? Could it be, as the Sumerians also claimed, these "gods" were flesh and blood beings from another planet in our solar system? And if so, is it possible that another planet in our solar system could have eluded science this long?

Interestingly, in addition to the Sumerian claims, we also know from other ancient cultures, like the Egyptians and Babylonians that the tenth planet really exists! In fact, they warn that its gravitational forces cause havoc here on Earth every time it passes by.

Today, while the scientific position is that the tenth planet does not exist, from time to time modern astronomers seem to reverse their position on this subject, and every so often they begin a new search to locate the mysterious Planet X, as we call it today. And what causes the scientific opinion to change from time to time?

Those not keeping up with scientific discoveries should know that we found planet Uranus in 1781. Immediately after the discovery of Uranus, scientists noticed certain gravitational perturbations in the behavior of this planet, and that led them to believe that another big planet out there may be causing those anomalies. In 1846, that search led to the discovery of Neptune, and due to the same anomalies that were witnessed on Neptune, after a long search, we discovered Pluto in 1930. As Pluto's mass, though, was too small to cause such gravitational anomalies, scientists concluded that there must be another large celestial body in our solar system capable of producing these anomalies on Neptune. So while for the most part of the 20th century, mainstream science searched and debated the existence of a tenth planet, without having conclusive evidence or being able to fully explain the anomalies on the outer planets, for the most part they decided to abandon the search for planet X. So, the mystery still remains. Is there another planet in our solar system? According to the Sumerian texts and other ancient cultures, the answer is a very definite—yes! Not only does this planet exist, but in great detail, the Sumerians explain that Planet X is the home of the Anunnaki, the anthropomorphic gods who genetically created the human race in their image!

More specifically, and according to the Sumerian story of creation, these gods created mankind, not for some higher purpose but simply in need of viable work force here on Earth, able to sustain the Garden of "Edin" in Mesopotamia and to relieve the Anunnaki workers at the gold mines of South Africa. The Sumerian texts explain in detail that the Anunnaki needed enormous amounts of gold, enough to "correct" their planet's atmosphere!

A pure fantasy, some will say. Maybe, although the fact that modern science incidentally traces the origin of man in South Africa raises a few suspicions. And to make matters even more interesting, how else do we explain the prehistoric gold mines recently found in South Africa? Of course, it goes without saying that neither archaeology nor science can provide good answers for the existence of these mines, or why early men had this massive craving for gold, as if they were "pre-programmed" for it. What possibly could be the motive for our early ancestors to devote thousands of years of their primitive existence in the production of gold? Most importantly, where did the knowledge for such a mass-scale undertaking come from?

For man to pursue gold in such an early stage, it is as if the knowledge of gold mining coincided with the primary need for survival. And, even if for a moment we went along with such an assumption and agreed that primitive humans excavated the gold for themselves, what happened to all the prehistoric artifacts from such production? They all seem to have vanished!

Finally, there is another question we need to ask ourselves. How do we really explain our implied affiliation between God and gold? Such correlation is not only evident in "modern" religious texts, but since our recorded history, it seems that early humans attributed divine elements to gold, so much that various cultures were known to ingest gold for its godly powers. So while there are no scientific answers to many of these questions, is it possible to assume that there is something more in Sumerian claims?

How do we know so much about the Sumerians, though, one may ask? Actually, a vast amount of written texts were left behind by this culture. The Sumerians were not only obsessed in documenting their religious beliefs in great detail, but their laws and all aspects of their daily lives were also meticulously documented on clay tablets and cylinders that were carefully preserved. Essentially, excavations in the Mesopotamian region unearthed more than 20,000 such tablets and cylinder seals in cuneiform writing. A cylinder seal is actually a cylinder engraved with a "picture story" that was used to roll its impression on a flat sheet of wet clay.

As the Akkadians and Babylonians fell into the Sumerian footsteps and continued on the same customs and beliefs, when combining the material left behind by all three cultures, we have a wealth of information that amounts to over a million clay tablets!

The Sumerian culture and beliefs, though, did not only influence the Akkadians and Babylonians. As the Hebrews ultimately conquered the Mesopotamian region from the Babylonians around the 6th century BC, not only did they assimilate themselves into the Babylonian culture, but they began to copy and celebrate the same Sumerian religious beliefs as other cultures did before them for thousands of years. As the early Hebrew revered the Sumerian stories as "divine," many were translated and became a permanent fixture into the Old Testament of the Holy Bible! Indeed, when comparing the Sumerian texts to several stories in the Old Testament, the only difference between the two versions—other than the names of cities and characters that were changed during translation—is that the stories in the Bible are shorter and simpler versions of the Sumerian originals.

Interestingly enough, though, while Hebrew translators simplified some of these stories, "accidentally" they left behind so many elements from the original narrative that one cannot help but to notice the plagiarism committed. Among other things, for example, there are several suggestions of plurality when referring to God, as well as many references of God "searching" for gold!

Although Christianity with the coming of Christ officially became a "monotheistic" religion, most references to God in the Old Testament are copied exactly as in the Sumerian original and insinuate plurality of gods. So while such "errors" in the Old Testament are often explained away by the church, the Sumerian version of the same stories demands no interpretation.

According to the Sumerians, the gods, which they called Anunnaki, meaning "those who from the heaven came to Earth," were not some abstract deities they created in need of worship, but real flesh and blood outwardly beings with "supernatural" powers, who periodically lived among them and provided them with essential technology and helped them understand the creation of the cosmos. With the exception that these gods possessed the power of eternal life, the Sumerians depicted them to be very much humanlike and able to experience and feel every human emotion such as anger, sorrow, love, lust, regret, etc.

The Sumerian texts further explain that the Anunnaki came to Earth for the first time in need of gold during one of Nibiru's nearby orbits, more than 200,000 years ago and long before *Homo sapiens* existed. They landed in an ancient valley south of the Mesopotamia region, currently under the waters of the Persian Gulf, where initially they thought it was an area that contained enormous deposits of gold.

> Where there is gold; and the gold of that land is good…
> [17] (Genesis, 2:11–12.)

When studying the Earth's climate during the last half million years, it appears that, between 200,000 BC and 250,000 BC, when reportedly the Anunnaki created the first humans, the entire Persian Gulf was a dry valley due to a periodic ice age.

Sumerians further explain that once the Anunnaki landed, one of their primary tasks was to cultivate the land and to create a fertile "garden" that could support their extended stay here on Earth. This garden that the Sumerians referred to as Edin (in Sumerian it means "a fertile valley") was geographically located in an area within the Persian Gulf where four rivers (Tigris, Euphrates, Pishon, and Gihon) met into a single river that ultimately flowed through this prehistoric valley. Satellite imagery shows that the rivers Pishon and Gihon, dry riverbeds now, once flowed into the same direction as Tigris and Euphrates. If not for the now-flooded region of the Persian Gulf interrupting their original flow, all four would have once connected somewhere at the bottom of the Persian Gulf in a very shallow and fertile prehistoric valley.

For those not so familiar with the Bible, incidentally the location of the Sumerian Garden of Edin was precisely where the Old Testament places the Garden of Eden! Is this just a mere coincidence?

The following passage from the Bible not only confirms the geographic location of the garden, that incidentally matches the Sumerian story, but most importantly the two references of gold in the same paragraph hints that either the Hebrew God was also interested in gold or when this story was copied by the Hebrew, this small detail was accidentally left in.

> The name of the first is Pishon: that is it which compasseth the whole land of Havilah, where there is gold; and the gold of that land is good: there is bdellium and the onyx stone. And the name of the second river is Gihon: the same is it that compasseth the whole land of Cush…" And the name of the third is Hiddekel: that is it which goeth toward the east of Assyria. And the fourth river is Euphrates." [18] (Genesis 2:11–14.)

As the Bible asserts, "the whole land of Havilah, where there is gold" reiterates the importance of gold to God, while the second phrase "the gold of that land is good" further suggests that the mention of gold was not associated with a geographical location alone, but indeed gold had a particular value to God! This paragraph from the Old Testament reads as if God specifically were searching for an area rich in gold!

As unusual this hypothesis may sound though, it is not the only time gold is mentioned in the Bible. Below there are few more references of gold:

> And the gold of that land is good: there is bdellium and the onyx stone. [19] (Genesis 2:12.)

Take from among you a contribution to the Lord; whoever is of a willing heart, let him bring it as the Lord's
contribution: gold, silver, and bronze. [20] (Exodus 35:5.)

All the gold of the offering which they offered up to the
Lord, from the captains of thousands and the captains
of hundreds, was 16,750 shekels. [21] (Exodus 31:52.)

And they came, both men and women, as many as were
willing hearted, and brought bracelets, and earrings,
and rings, and tablets, all jewels of gold: and every man
that offered an offering of gold to the Lord." [22] (Exodus
31:22.)

The silver is mine, and the gold is mine, declares the
Lord Almighty. [23] (Haggai 2:8.)

So, while the Sumerians explain why gold was so valuable to the
gods, the Old Testament continues to emphasize the importance of
gold, but it provides no particular explanation why.

Gold, of course, is not the only reference in the Old Testament that
points to this plagiarism committed by the early Hebrew Christians. In
fact, when comparing the Bible stories to those of the Sumerian texts,
with the exception of more Hebrew-friendly names and a few other
minor variations, many of them seem to be nearly identical. For example, the Sumerian version of Genesis, referred to as Eridu, explains that
in the beginning the divine spirits created the universe. Following the
creation of the universe, on the first day, the gods created light; the
second day, the firmament above; on the third day, it was the dry land;
the fourth day, all the heavenly lights; the next day, they created man;
and finally, on the last day, the gods rested.

Although both stories of creation as described in Genesis and
Eridu sound extremely similar, Christian scholars will quickly point
that Christianity is a monotheistic religion while the Sumerian faith
that is referring to gods in plural is clearly a polytheistic faith.

Unfortunately for the Christian scholars though, the following verse from the Book of Genesis brings that claim under a closer scrutiny:

> And God said, let us make man in our image, after our likeness: and let them have dominion over the fish of the sea, and over the fowl of the air, and over the cattle, and over all the earth, and over every creeping thing that creeps upon the earth. [24] (Genesis 1:26.)

Just as in the Sumerian story where the gods met to announce their decision to create the first human in *their* image and likeness, the above description from Genesis, ("let *us*," "in *our* image," "after *our* likeness") not only insinuates plurality but also embraces the original Sumerian version. Was this just another mistake of the early Hebrew translators?

These, of course, are not the only similarities that suggest plurality. Often enough, throughout the Old Testament, and just like the Sumerian stories do, God continues to refer to himself as being many:

> Then the Lord God said, "Behold, the man has become like one of us, knowing good and evil; and now, lest he stretch out his hand, and take also from the tree of life, and eat, and live forever." [25] (Genesis 3:22.)

Once again, the phrase "one of *us*" insinuates more than one deity is present. In fact, the references of plurality are so many, when the Bible is read in the form that it is written, without any attempts to insert meanings of singularity in what we read, another story (the original Sumerian story), emerges right before us.

And the similarities go on. According to the original story, once the gods created man in their image, (and by the way, the Sumerian version explains that there were several attempts and failures prior to success), the newly created humans were placed in the garden of Edin, and just as in the Christian faith, they were given instructions to maintain it.

And the Lord God took the man, and put him into the Garden of Eden to dress it and to keep it. [26] (Genesis 2:15.)

A significant difference between the two stories though, is that the Sumerian version clearly admits that man was simply created so he can literally serve the gods as a mere laborer, where Christianity, although the orders given were the same, placed another more abstract meaning to particular words. A "servant" of God became someone who praises God while specific instructions given to man by God to "dress and till the land" were interpreted by Christian scholars as if this was for the benefit of man and not God. And while the Christian Church will never accept that the Hebrew God intended to use humans as mere laborers, the story in the Bible actually hints otherwise.

Unlike the many plural remarks found throughout the Old Testament that we are told to either ignore—or better yet— alter the meaning in order to have a more spiritual consequence, the original Sumerian story appears to be more straightforward.

The Sumerian texts explain further that all gods were not equal. Anu was the father deity who ultimately returned to planet Nibiru. Enki (initially in charge of Earthly matters) and Enlil (in charge of the sky) were "rival" brothers. Ninhursanga was Enki's half-sister. All other Anunnaki, as the Sumerians explain, although still very powerful, did not have any authority, and they were primarily here on Earth to work the mines and follow directions. When comparing this class structure to the "modern" Christian beliefs, doesn't this depiction resemble the same hierarchy of an almighty father-figure God who is surrounded by his Son, Mary, the Holy Spirit, several archangels, and many more less powerful angels? Is this just a coincidence? In fact, when you bring Lucifer into the mix, another "spiritual" entity so powerful and so "equal" to God that in essence "rivals" God himself, then we have a story that is nearly identical: Two rival brothers fighting for the fate of mankind.

The Sumerian texts further explain that for several millennia, after their arrival here on Earth, the Anunnaki continued to excavate for gold in the Mesopotamia region, although ultimately they were not able to produce the results the god Anu had expected. As their initial effort to recover sufficient amount of gold was noted as a failure, Anu demoted Enki and placed Enlil in charge of the entire operation with new instructions to relocate the mining from the Mesopotamia region to South Africa, where higher deposits of gold were thought to exist. So it was done. The Anunnaki operation along with the entire human workforce moved from Edin to a region of South Africa referred to in the Sumerian texts as Abzu. From there, the precious metal was carried back to Edin, and from Mesopotamia, it was regularly shipped to their planet.

Is this another strange coincidence, or do the Sumerians offer an explanation on how and why the human species appeared to have "emerged" out of South Africa? Moreover, how do we explain the Sumerian assertion that South Africa was rich in gold? Could these details be a mere coincidence or one lucky guess after another by the Sumerians? How could a 6000 year-old civilization concoct such a fantastic story where every piece of the puzzle seems to fit! If the gold deposits of South Africa and the particular ancient mines evaded modern detection until recently, how could the Sumerians know of their existence?

In our quest for answers, one thing is certain. Without the Sumerian explanation, the prehistoric mines of South Africa should not exist! Our modern theory of creation and evolution, especially human development, heavily contradicts their existence. Gold (to early humans) would have been useless. As gold is too soft for tools and weapons, it would have been absolutely worthless to a primitive hunter and gatherer human. The existence of these primitive mines simply challenge all scientific explanations, as clearly they could not have existed during our prehistory. Could it be then that the Sumerians were right all along in their assertions? Obviously, gold is a much more valuable commodity to a modern society like ours, or that of the Anunnaki for that matter. Just like the aluminum oxide, which some claim today is sprayed into the Earth's stratosphere in order to deflect the Sun's energy and prevent global warming, is it possible that a substantial quantity of gold micro-particles in a wondering planet's thermosphere, can amplify light, while at the same time, protect that planet from harmful radiation and help retain some of its heat?

NASA today, extensively uses gold in space equipment for several reasons. Gold is resistant to corrosion and is a stable lubricant. Unlike gold—which is stable—most other lubricants quickly breakdown when in space, especially under extreme radiation. Gold is also used to reflect harmful heat from thrusters and engines, thus protecting equipment and personnel in the interior of a cabin. Gold is able to reflect visible light, so a thin layer of gold used on the astronauts' helmets helps reduce glare and protects them from harmful radiation. Finally, gold is the most malleable and ductile of all metals. It can be pounded into thin sheets without breaking, and it can be drawn into thin wires without snapping. Gold, without a doubt, is more useful to an advanced society than a primitive one.

According to the Sumerian texts, for thousands of years after their arrival, the Anunnaki gods excavated the gold themselves until the Anunnaki working class began to resent the harsh conditions associated with it. To avoid a rebellion, Enki—a scientist god and the architect of Edin—devised a plan and proposed to the other hierarchy of gods that they should solve their problem by creating a primitive worker to take the place of the Anunnaki worker. He would be a creature that would literally serve the gods while here on Earth.

> Fashion servants for the Gods… [27] (Enuma Elish.)

When the other gods asked how he was planning to achieve this, Enki answered,

> The creature whose name thou has uttered, it exists, bind upon it the "mark" of the Gods… [28] (Enuma Elish.)

After much trial and error—and according to Sumerians, there were many failures—in the end, they succeeded in incorporating the blood from one of the gods with that of a hominid species from Earth, thus genetically creating the first human by combining terrestrial with extraterrestrial DNA.

As fantastic or even shocking as this story may sound, in reality this 6000 year-old account provides the best explanation yet for where the extra 223 "mystery" genes in the human evolution came from! This claim not only explains the mystery of the missing link, but it also helps to fill in several other gaps that exist in the Old Testament. In fact, with this explanation in place, we now fully understand why and how man was fashioned in the image of his creator.

Furthermore, is it possible that the mention of the phrase "flesh and blood," that so commonly is used by the Christian Church, could be none other but a reference to the Sumerian story of creation when gods literally incorporated in us their flesh and blood (their DNA, in essence), thus elevating the status of an earthly creature into a higher state of being and closer to its creator? Not only does this claim better explain the origin of the phrase "flesh and blood," but it also raises the question whether early Hebrew Christians, including Jesus himself, knew of this literal transformation; thus it was the reasoning behind the famous symbolism during the Last Supper.

> For I received from the Lord what I also passed on to you: The Lord Jesus, on the night he was betrayed, took bread, and when he had given thanks, he broke it and said, "This is my body, which is for you; do this in remembrance of me." In the same way, after supper he took the cup, saying, "This cup is the new covenant in my blood; do this, whenever you drink it, in remembrance of me." [29] (Corinthians 11:23–26.)

Although Christians tend to believe that Christ, during the Last Supper, was the first ever to symbolically compare "bread and wine" to his "flesh and blood," is it possible that he was only commemorating past knowledge; and in essence, his act during the Last Supper was in remembrance of the genetic creation described in the Sumerian story of creation? Could this be a simple misunderstanding by modern Christians that most often tend to change various words, and their literal meaning, to something more elusive?

If anything, it appears that there are several places in the Bible where the meaning of a particular word is interpreted otherwise, or the actual text was clearly misunderstood during translation from one language to another. For example, the Christian belief that God created

Adam out of the earth, as in soil, literally could be better explained with the Sumerian tale that claims gods created the "Adamu "(in Sumerian, "human" in plural) while combining their "blood" with a creature "from Earth" (and not "of earth" as in dirt). As the word *earth* describes the name of our planet as well as the earth we walk on, isn't it possible that the Hebrew translators misinterpreted the procedure and the elements involved?

"Far-fetched hypothesis" some may say. Actually, when dissecting and studying the root of the name Adam, the name itself strengthens this hypothesis further. In Hebrew, the word-name *Adam* is a child root derived from the parent meaning "blood." When examining a few other words that derive from the same Hebrew child root, we can also see a common meaning among all of them. The Hebrew word *Adamah*, for example, is the feminine form meaning "Earth." The word *dam* also means "red" (as in red blood). So when the Hebrew version of the story claims that Adam was formed out of the Adamah, it is clearly a misinterpretation of the original Sumerian claim that explains how gods mixed their DNA (or "red blood" for lack of better words) with a creature *from* Earth (Earth as the planet and not off earth as in dirt). Binding the "blood" of the gods to a creature *from* Earth was always the original assertion made, while it appears that the Hebrew and others who copied the same story, eventually lost that message during translation.

Another Christian belief that could also be a misconception is God's "breath of life" as interpreted by many religious scholars. God's breathing life into the first man may not be a description of an actual act but a creative expression that further describes a God-granting-life act and a special connection between man and his creator. This poetic depiction best describes the biblical view of what it means to be human and best describes the close relationship of man with his creator. Animation or "breath of life," if you will, poetically portrays the extension of God in man's existence.

One more interesting Sumerian aspect that coincides with Christianity and further explains the relationship of the serpent to Lucifer is that according to the Sumerian depictions, Enki's symbol was the serpent. Ironically, the symbol of the god responsible for creating mankind and the Garden of Edin was often depicted as two serpents twisting around each other, much like the modern symbol of medicine, or better yet, a DNA double helix.

Could it be that Enki, the Sumerian serpent god, and later the biblical serpent, known as Lucifer, were ultimately the same deities who caused Adam and Eve to be expelled from the garden?

Those who still don't see the link should know that the meaning of the name Lucifer, in Greek as well as in Latin, translates to "him who brings the light" or to someone who enlightens! According to the Sumerian version, after Enki created man, he provided him with knowledge. In fact, the Sumerian story explains that humans were expelled from the garden after the god Enki convinced them that they were better off free than serving the gods as mere laborers. Could it be then that Enki, ironically, was the misinterpreted "evil" serpent in the Bible who persuaded Adam and Eve to eat from the tree of knowledge, thus ultimately helping man to their misinterpreted freedom?

Enlil, on the other hand, the god in command of the Annunaki and now of all Earthly matters, from the very beginning was not so fond of the human race. He was worried that humanity will ultimately explode out of control, and according to the Sumerians, he is the punishing god who always wanted the human race destroyed at every opportunity.

Two deities are fighting for the fate of the human race! Is this starting to sound like the ongoing battles between good and evil, God and Lucifer, as we know them in Christianity? One part of "God" wants humanity's destruction, while another part of "God"—at the same time—protects humanity from total annihilation.

Is it possible that even more details in the original story could have gotten twisted during translation from Babylonian to Hebrew? For example, the "single deity" as interpreted in the Hebrew and Christian religions, contradicts itself so much that it puzzles even some theologians! Why does the Judean-Christian God appear to have a split personality? Why does he, in one chapter, appear to be loving and protective toward his creation; while at other times, he wants to eliminate mankind? And why does the Judean-Christian God, just as in the Sumerian version, refer to himself as a dual entity?

Once more, as the stories in the Old Testament are clearly copies, the behavior of the Judean-Christian God resembles that of the

Sumerian gods where Enki was the loving god and Enlil the punishing god.

Those who still don't see the resemblance between the two and insist that the Old Testament characterizes a monotheistic religion, should also consider the following: In the original Hebrew version of the Old Testament, and before the early texts were ultimately translated to several more "Westernized" versions, the name of God is mentioned often as Elohim. Of course, the word *Elohim* in Hebrew refers to concepts of divinity, but there is one big problem with this word. Although according to religious scholars Elohim should refer to a singular God, it poses a clear contradiction as the word has a plural meaning. For example, when used, it truly means "angels, gods, deities," etc. So once again, this not only corroborates the similarities between the Christian and Sumerian versions, but it reinforces the plurality aspect when comparing the two stories!

By the way, the frequent comparison to the Hebrew Bible is necessary because it contains the "original" biblical story as it was first written and before any modern translation took place. This original Hebrew version of the Bible, along with the Eastern Greek Orthodox version that was recorded and coexisted about the same time, are widely considered the only two remaining original Bible versions. In effect, according to these two Christian sects, it is considered heretic to allow the original texts to be translated and/or for the Bible to be studied as divine material once translation takes place. They claim, and understandably so, that from one translation to another, especially centuries later, the original story and its true meaning will ultimately be "lost in translation." So unlike the modern-day Bibles, especially those used in Western Europe and United States that have been repeatedly interpreted over the centuries, it is inconceivable for these two groups to allow any revisions in their original texts—even if it means that, by doing so, they could avoid embarrassing comparisons.

So ultimately, when the Sumerian texts are placed side by side with the Old Testament, it immediately becomes clear to the reader that Christianity, the newer of the two versions, heavily borrowed from the original Sumerian source. When keeping in mind though that many of the founding fathers of Christianity were either born or lived in ancient Mesopotamia during the period when the Sumerian faith ruled, it is not surprising to see that the Hebrew did what the Akkadian and Babylonian cultures did before them. They copied from the Sumerian texts. Of course, by changing the names of the cities and characters, they made these stories more Hebrew friendly.

Let's take the story of the Great Flood, for example. According to the Sumerian version of Genesis, the god Enki warns Ziudsura (the Sumerian Noah) that the gods decided to destroy humanity and that he needed to build an ark in order to save himself, his family, and their animals. The similarities in the description of the events are striking. Both stories share the following identical points:

- Genesis, as well as the Babylonian "Epic of Gilgamesh" explain that mankind lost their moral values and they were to be destroyed by the God (or gods).
- The god(s) decided to cause a worldwide flood that destroyed mankind.
- In both cases, the gods (or god) warned and saved a righteous man named Ut-Napishtim, or Noah if you prefer.
- In both cases, the hero of the story was told to save self as well as few others by escaping the flood in a multilevel wooden ark.
- Along with humans, samples of animals were loaded into the ark.
- The ark had many internal compartments.
- According to both descriptions, the ark had a single door and at least one window.
- With the exception that the Bible claims the incident took 40 days and nights, the event in Gilgamesh took seven days. Both stories, of course, talk about a cataclysmic flood that covered the Earth with water.
- The ark ultimately landed on the peak of a mountain, somewhere in the Middle East.
- The hero sends out birds in intervals to help him determine if dry land was in the near vicinity. In both stories, the first two birds returned, while the third found dry land and did not return.

- In both stories, the hero and his family sacrifice an animal to the God (or gods).
- The gods, or God if you prefer, smelled the aroma of the roasted animal.
- Both stories also portray the God (or gods) having regretted their action to destroy humanity and promised not to do this again.

Interestingly enough, familiar similarities exist also when comparing the Sumerian version to the story of the biblical Tower of Babel.

Just as in the Bible, mankind had one language, until due to their growing arrogance, God confounded their tongues. The following Sumerian story that contains similar elements is also preserved in "Enmerkar and the Lord of Aratta":

> On that day when there is no snake, when there is no scorpion, when there is no hyena, when there is no lion, when there is neither dog nor wolf, when there is thus neither fear nor trembling, man has no rival! At such a time, may the lands of Shubur and Hamazi, the harmonious (?)—tongued, and Sumer, the great mountain of the me of magnificence, and Akkad, the land possessing all that is befitting, and the Martu land, resting in security—the whole universe, the well-guarded people—may they all address Enlil together in a single language! For at that time, for the ambitious lords, for the ambitious princes, for the ambitious kings, Enki, the lord of abundance and of steadfast decisions, the wise and knowing lord of the Land, the expert of the gods, chosen for wisdom, the lord of Eridu, shall change the speech in their mouths, as many as he had placed there, and so the speech of mankind is truly one. [30]

The Bible, of course, confirms that the Tower of Babel was actually in ancient Babylonia while the ancient Greek researcher and historian Herodotus of Halicarnassus, when describing the temple that still existed in his time, and during the 5th century BC, said the following:

The temple of Bêl, the Babylonian Zeus… was still in existence in my time. It has a solid central tower, one stadium square, with a second erected on top of it and then a third, and so on up to eight. All eight towers can be climbed by a spiral way running round the outside, and about half way up there are seats for those who make the ascent to rest on. On the summit of the topmost tower stands a great temple with a fine large couch in it, richly covered, and a golden table beside it. The shrine contains no image, and no one spends the night there except (if we may believe that Chaldaeans who are the priests of Bêl) one Babylonian woman, all alone, whoever it may be that the god has chosen. The Chaldaeans also say—though I do not believe them—that the god enters the temple in person and takes his rest upon the bed. [31]

Herodotus' description clearly depicts a Babylonian Ziggurat, a man-made brick structure that resembled a step pyramid with a temple resting over the top. In this case, all the evidence shows that the Temple of Etemenanki was the Tower of Babel. According to ancient descriptions, the square structure measured 91 by 91 meters at the base, while its height was also estimated at 91 meters. Unfortunately, according to historians, this temple was dismantled by Alexander the Great in an attempt to rebuild it. Of course, with his death following soon after, the reconstruction never took place.

Another Mesopotamian tale resembles that of biblical Moses. The original story talks about Sargon of Akkad, also known as Sargon the Great, who was the first king and founder of Babylon. In the story of Sargon (2379 BC to 2215 BC), which was written long before the story of Moses, his mother similarly placed him in a basket to flow down the river, hoping that someone will find the infant and raise him as their own. A Neo-Assyrian text from the 7th century BC, and one of the newer finds that attest to the story of Sargon, describes the following:

My mother was a high priestess, my father I knew not.
The brothers of my father loved the hills. My city is

Azupiranu, which is situated on the banks of the Euphrates. My high priestess mother conceived me, in secret she bore me. She set me in a basket of rushes with bitumen she sealed my lid. She cast me into the river which rose over me. The river bore me up and carried me to Akki, the drawer of water. Akki, the drawer of water, took me as his son and reared me. Akki, the drawer of water, appointed me as his gardener. While I was a gardener, Ishtar granted me her love, and for four and… years I exercised kingship. [32]

It is evident that, in both stories, the infant is found and ultimately in adulthood became a hero of its people. In Sargon's story, he becomes a mighty warrior who helps establish the Akkadian Empire, while Moses leads his people out of bondage.

A significant difference in the two stories is that the legend of Sargon is not only found in actual manuscripts dating around the 7th century BC, but crucial elements of the Sargon story were noted thousands of years before that. Unlike the Sargon legend, the Moses story first appeared in Hebrew manuscripts between the 2nd and 3rd centuries BC. Nothing about Moses exists before this time.

Another biblical tale that was possibly inspired from the Babylonians is the story of the Ten Commandments. Just like the Hebrew story that followed much later, in the Babylonian version, God gives the tablets that contain the "code of law" to Hammurabi, the sixth king of Babylon. Interestingly enough, this code of law that became the law of the land for thousands of years, heavily subscribed on an "eye for an eye" and "tooth for tooth" philosophy! Suspiciously enough, this was also the premise of the Old Testament until Jesus and the New Testament came along.

Once again, while knowing that the Hebrews operated on the same set of laws practiced by the Sumerians, isn't it then possible to assume that not only the Ten Commandments story may have been inspired by the earlier Babylonian story, but in fact, the "eye for an eye" premise that so heavily dominated in the Old Testament—a position that heavily contradicted the teachings of Christ and more specifically the principle of "turning the other cheek" was also based on Sumerian laws, as well?

So is the revelation that the Old Testament is essentially a copy of another much older original, a good reason to dismiss and abandon the Old Testament of the Bible altogether? On the contrary, why should we discard a textbook that so far appears to have been historically valid! On the flip side though, if the "copied" account of the two versions already proved its historical significance, isn't it time, perhaps, to pay closer attention to the original account? In doing so, is it conceivable to assume that the gods of antiquity may have genetically created the human race in need of a labor force? And if so, what about their involvement afterwards? Have they continued to get involved in human affairs, as the Sumerians and the Bible asserts? Every culture on our planet actually would go along with the notion that "divine beings" always have done that. If so, then what power or type of "arsenal" did these "spiritual entities" have in their possession that could annihilate entire cities as if by "brimstone and fire"?

# THE TECHNOLOGY AND THE FLYING MACHINES OF THE GODS

*The Flying Machines of Ancient India, 500BC --
Atomic Detonations Recorded in Antiquity? -- Jet
Planes in South America 1500 Years Ago? -- Did
Alexander the Great Encounter UFO's? -- Did
Prophet Ezekiel Witness God or a UFO?*

The Mahabharata and Ramayana, two major epics written prior to the 5th century BC, are essentially detailed Hindu stories that contain religious teachings, customs, morality, history, and legends concerning the gods and heroes of ancient India. They are often compared to Homer's epics, Iliad and Odyssey; although with 1.8 million words in the Mahabharata alone, this epic is ten times bigger than both Iliad and Odyssey combined.

Along with their philosophical and moral teachings, the Mahabharata contains a narrative of the Kurukshetra War and its outcome. The story concludes with the death of Lord Krishna, the end of his dynasty and the ascent of the Pandava brothers to heaven. It also marks the beginning of Kali Yuga, the fourth and final age of mankind, in which man is headed toward the complete dissolution of values and morality.

What is most fascinating about these manuscripts, though, is not their classic depiction of an older world, but their depiction of an ancient world with flying machines, as well as technology and weapon systems that surpass even that of the 21$^{st}$ century! The stories often talk about internal combustion engines and "double-deck aircrafts with many windows" that could "race into the sky until they appear to look like comets," or airships that "soar into the regions of both the sun and the stars." They refer to these flying machines as Vimanas, and the texts go on to describe their construction, their required maintenance, and they provide some sort of "flying manual" for their successful operation.

The texts also explain that there were several types of Vimana aircrafts, some smaller with single engines and some larger with several engines. They describe their fuel as a "yellowish-white liquid" or a "compound of mercury" and talk about their ability to lift vertically and move in any direction, as intended by their pilot, while during lift-off, a roaring flame shot out of them.

> In the central container is the liquid consumed by the engine, which gradually burns away during complete combustion. Fully renowned is the conquering of the following motions: Vertical ascent; vertical descent; forwards; backwards; normal ascent; normal descent; slanting; progressing over long distances, through proper adjustment of the working parts... its air-rending sound and roaring thunder can easily drown out the trumpeting of an elephant in panic—but it can also be moved by musical tones. [33]

> Thus, inside one must place the Mercury-engine; and properly mounted beneath it, the iron heating apparatus. Men thusly set the dual-winged, driving whirlwind in motion; and the concealed pilot, by means of the

mercury-power, may travel a great distance in the sky… Into the interior structure four strong mercury containers must be installed. When these have been heated by a controlled fire from iron containers, the flying machine develops thunder-power through the mercury, becoming a highly desirable yantra… if this iron engine with properly welded joints be filled with fluid, when ascending or descending over land it generates power with the roar of a lion. [34]

Descriptions of these machines, though, do not end with their physical construction or flying characteristics, but most interestingly, with their weapon systems and how frightfully they seem similar to weapons of modern times.

According to these texts, Vimanas could destroy another object or a structure with a beam of light, or they could annihilate an entire army or a city with an "iron thunderbolt," a "single projectile charged with all the power of the universe" that when detonated caused "an incandescent column of smoke and fire to rise" and a blast that was "bright as a thousand suns"!

Nothing could withstand the power of such a weapon, not even the gods according to the texts:

(It was) a single projectile charged with all the power of the universe. An incandescent column of smoke and flame as bright as a thousand suns rose in all its splendor… it was an unknown weapon, an iron thunderbolt, a gigantic messenger of death, which reduced to ashes the entire race of the Vrishnis and the Andhakas… the corpses were so burned as to be unrecognizable. The hair and nails fell out; pottery broke without apparent cause, and the birds turned white. After few hours all foodstuffs were infected… to escape from this fire the soldiers threw themselves in streams to wash themselves and their equipment. [35]

As inconceivable as the assertion of a nuclear detonation during antiquity, without a doubt, the above description resembles the atomic explosions of Hiroshima and Nagasaki and the effects they had on people and property. An explosion and a column of smoke that is bright as a "thousand suns" and powerful enough to wipe out an entire race? Corpses of people burn beyond recognition, food supplies "infected," and survivors washing themselves from what appears to be radioactive fallout? As fantastic as this comparison may sound to some, interestingly enough, on July 16, 1945 when Dr. Oppenheimer, the director of the Manhattan Project, witnessed the test explosion of the first atomic bomb, he later said that he could not help but to compare the modern atomic detonation to the descriptions in the Bhagavad Gita.

In other passages, the epics continue to describe the horrific power of these weapons that scorched men, horses, elephants, and chariots into "dry leaves," and "they looked like birds flying off the trees in a strong wind!" And while amazingly these detonations resemble modern atomic blasts, more incredibly so, the after-effects also resemble the aftermath of an atomic explosion.

> Winds, dry and strong, and showering gravels, blew from every side... Birds began to wheel, making circles from right to left... Meteors, showering (blazing) coals, fell on the Earth from the sky... The Suns disc... seemed to be always covered with dust... Fierce circles of light were seen every day around both the Sun and the Moon. These circles showed three hues. Their edges seemed to be black and rough and ashy-red in color. [36]

It is no wonder that, during the British occupation of India, when Western scholars for the first time began to study these ancient manuscripts, they could not recognize the technological similarities. During the Victorian era, when for the first time the Mahabharata and Ramayana came to light among the Western world, the Wright Brothers had not yet invented flight, and atomic detonations did not take place for another 100 years.

Is it possible that the author of these epics just imagined such technology, or could he have witnessed it? Is it possible that these depictions were several "lucky" guesses, or should we assume the possibility that the "gods" may have used this technology in our distant past?

Actually, as it seems, the flying machines described in the Mahabharata were not the only flying machines our ancestors ever witnessed. Ancient relics of model jet airplanes were found in South America, as well! Could these be the same vehicles described in Mahabharata and Ramayana? Not only do they appear to have the shape of a modern jetplane, but they are clearly equipped with horizontal and vertical tail stabilizers, a characteristic that does not exist in nature or in insects or moths, as some skeptics' claim those could be.

In truth, these tiny artifacts not only look like modern airplanes, but they fly like real airplanes, as a couple of researchers from the AAS-RA (Archaeology Astronautics and SETI research Association) already proved. When two of these crafts were enlarged to scale and retrofitted with a propeller and a small jet engine, once tested, both flew and maneuvered just like modern airplanes.

So what is that mean? Did our ancestors 1,500 years ago create these models just to demonstrate to future generations that they had the knowledge of flight, in theory at least; or did they really witness these machines in action? In fact, the yellowish-white liquid described in the Mahabharata sounds more like gasoline used by pulse-jet engines. Mercury compound, on the other hand, has been used successfully by NASA for ion propulsion systems since 1964 by SERT 1 (Space Electric Rocket Test). In 1970, a second test, SERT 2 verified the operation of two mercury ion thrusters for thousands of running hours.

Currently, a NASA spacecraft sent out to explore Ceres and Vesta—the two dwarf planets in the Asteroid Belt—use ion-engine thrusters. The *Dawn* spacecraft took off from Cape Canaveral atop a Delta 2 rocket in September of 2007. It already completed its mission studying Vesta and, if all goes well, is scheduled to arrive at Ceres in February 2015.

In other tests, not as conclusive yet, especially in the eyes of the general public, scientists use mercury in their research for an antigravity propulsion system that works on the premise of a rotating liquid metal.

As bizarre as this may sound, reportedly, just before the end of World War 2, the Nazis were also experimenting with antigravity technology that rotated a mercury-like substance in a top-secret project code named The Bell (*Die Glocke* in German). The Bell Project was so important to the Germans that, in order to push its completion before the end of the war, they put all their resources in it and reportedly abandoned all other research projects, including their research on atomic weapons. The Bell was the weapon of their choice and one that they believed could help them end the war in their favor!

Knowing this, is it possible to assume that the Third Reich could have been experimenting on technological remnants discovered in one of their many expeditions to India or Tibet? Why else were Hitler and the Nazis were so interested in those ancient manuscripts? Historically, it is widely documented that since the 1930s (if not earlier) the Nazis were aggressively sending scientific expeditions to India and Tibet in search of relics, and with intent to further study the ancient Hindu scriptures.

It is speculated that the adaptation of the counter clockwise swastika by the Nazi party in the 1920s, and ultimately the incorporation of the swastika on the Nazi flag, a prime symbol of Nazi power, was also influenced by the clockwise swastika that is linked to the mysterious Indus Valley Civilization that flourished 4,000 years ago. This, in effect, was the same civilization depicted in the Mahabharata and Ramayana and the one the Germans were so intrigued by. So what was so fascinating about this particular civilization? Did the Nazis discover a relic in India's ancient past that made them want to go back for more? As circumstantial as this hypothesis might be, why their fascination with certain ancient Hindu "fairy tales" and why did the German "Bell" suspiciously have the conical shape and characteristics of a Vimana, as described in the Mahabharata and Ramayana?

In the year 2000, a book written by Igor Witkowski named *The Truth about the Wonder Weapon* refers to the Nazi "Bell" in great detail.

Witkowski wrote that he discovered about this top-secret weapon in 1997, when he read original manuscripts from the interrogation of former Nazi SS Officer Jacob Sporrenberg, who was linked to the German secret Bell Project. The Nazi experiment that was supposed to end the war in favor of Hitler was carried out in a facility known as *Der Riese* (The Giant), near the Wenceslaus mine and very close to the Czech border.

The Bell was described as an object "made of a hard heavy metal," approximately 9 feet wide, more than 12 feet in height, and having the shape of a cone or bell. The device contained two counter-rotating cylinders which were filled with a mercury-like substance, violet in color.

Although no one knows for sure what type of weapon the "Bell" was, later authors and researchers speculated further that the Nazi project ended up in United States and as part of an agreement made with SS General Hans Kammler. Although to this day, the whereabouts of Kammler or place and date of his death remain unknown, some speculate he died in United States many years later. Some researchers also claimed that the Bell experiment continued in the hands of the United States, and the bell-shaped object that was recovered in 1965 by the military in the so-called "Kecksburg UFO Incident" was none other but an object from this program.

So as the flying machines described in the Mahabharata and Ramayana sounded like real mechanical devices, could we dare to assume that the Nazis got lucky in one of their many "scientific" expeditions, and before the end of the war, they discovered and worked on reverse engineering a machine that was originally used by the "gods of antiquity"? If so, that means, our experimentation with impulse gravity generators and antigravity propulsion systems today may be nothing but reinvention, if not "borrowed" technology used by the "gods" thousands of years ago.

What about other reports and descriptions of flying machines from ancient cultures like the Greeks and the Egyptians? Can some of these be reports of actual flying vehicles? Evidently, as it seems, every culture on our planet, at one point in history or another, reported flying machines.

Even the Hebrew Christians reported sightings of "whirlwind machines" that somehow they associated with God. Is it possible to assume that, in essence, all these people described the same technology or possibly even the same deities depicted in the Mahabharata? And if so, is it possible to assume that approximately 4000 years ago the annihilation of Mohenjo Daro and Harappa, as well as that of Sodom and Gomorra (otherwise known as Bab-edh-Dhra and Numeira), was by the same weapons?

Archaeological evidence certainly points that Mohenjo Daro and Harappa, as well as that of Sodom and Gomorrah, not only were similarly destroyed by an "unknown force," but the conditions in the aftermath were such that these cities were forever abandoned not only by the survivors but by all future generations.

The city ruins of Mohenjo Daro (translates "Mount of the Dead") and Harappa, are both approximately 4,000 years old and from historical accounts we know they prospered during the same period along with the Egyptians, the Minoans, and other Mesopotamian civilizations. Both were large, modern cities, relatively speaking, with brick structures reaching up to three stories in height, and at their peak, each city housed more than 30,000 inhabitants.

What is so strange about these two particular cities though is that around 1800 BC, and for a reason unknown, they were both abandoned. While mainstream archaeologists can only speculate as to what motivated these people to leave everything behind, Hindu legends explain that the occupants of these cities were warned to flee before certain destruction. And while archaeologists are still unable to explain why these cities were deserted or how they were ultimately destroyed, recent excavations at Mohenjo Daro raise more questions than provide answers.

It appears that the few dozen skeletal remains ever found were left in the streets where it seems they perished. No arrowheads or weapons of any kind were ever found to indicate that they were involved in a battle. No signs of physical conflict and no corpses of an opposing army were ever discovered. Moreover, the position of the skeletal remains found indicated that the fatal moment was swift and with very little warning.

What happened there remains a mystery. Why were the bodies of the dead left in the streets without a proper burial? Why did wild animals not feed on the remains and scatter the bones? And most importantly, what happened to all the survivors? Why did they not eventually return to reclaim their properties and to rebuild their homes? In fact, why did these cities remain permanently abandoned until their discovery nearly 4,000 years later? What horror could have gotten into those people that forced them to leave their possessions and livelihoods behind, including loved ones, and never look back? Were the people of

Mohenjo Daro and Harappa warned not to return and simply obeyed, or is it possible the conditions did not allow for their return?

Actually, recent tests conducted may confirm the latter assumption. Higher than normal traces of radiation, found among the ruins and on human remains, indicate that the cities may have been radioactive subsequent to their destruction. Further analysis also revealed that the mysterious black and green stones found near the ruins (Trinitite), were actually pottery fragments fused together after exposure to a high heat source. Today, such conditions are most commonly found around meteor impacts or nuclear test sites where stones are found to fuse together when exposed to a detonation that produces heat between 1,400–1,600 degrees centigrade (nearly 3,000 degrees Fahrenheit).

Is it possible, then, that Mohenjo Daro and Harappa are the cities described in the Bhagavad Gita? As mind-blowing as the assertion of an atomic blast in antiquity, what other weapon could have instantly annihilated Mohenjo Daro while imposing such effects on people and property? In fact, what weapon could have destroyed the cities of Sodom and Gomorra as if by "brimstone and fire" while leaving behind traces of radiation? Is it possible that the "wrath" of god described in the Bible is none other than the same type of technology and weapons of mass destruction depicted in the ancient Hindu texts?

According to written accounts, in 326 BC, when Alexander the Great crossed the Hydaspes River to engage the Hindu army in an effort to capture India, the conflict was temporarily interrupted by flying objects, described by Alexander's historian as "gleaming silver shields." Reportedly, these objects swooped down from the sky, and with several passes over the battlefield, not only caused panic amongst the war animals of both armies, but literally disrupted the initial confrontation. Although, ultimately, the battle was fought and won by the Greeks, Alexander decided not to advance further into India. Why though? Were the Greeks really "exhausted" as modern historians report, or is it possible that the unexplained incident convinced the Greeks and Alexander to alter their plans? Is it possible that the flying vehicles that caused the annihilation of Mohenjo Daro and Harappa within the immediate vicinity were the same kind of flying objects noted by Alexander's army nearly 1,500 years later? Is it conceivable to assume that Alexander was about to cross into a "forbidden" territory, thus the warning from the gods and their "gleaming silver shields"? Although no one will ever know for certain why, after this incident, the Greeks abandoned the Indian campaign, and they returned to Persia.

As surprising this story may sound, incredibly enough, it was not the only time Alexander's army had an encounter with unidentified flying objects. This time, it was during their attempt to capture the Phoenician city of Tyre, an island city with massive walls that proved to be one of Alexander's greatest challenges. In order to reach this island city, nearly half a mile offshore, for six months the Greeks became involved in the construction of a causeway that would allow them to reach its walls on foot, only ultimately to realize the walls were not only too tall, but also too thick to overcome with their seize equipment. After several failed attempts to breach the massive walls, and just when they thought they were facing the impossible, Alexander's chief historian noted that two flying objects appeared in the sky, and one of these objects destroyed a section of the wall with a "beam of light." With a section of the wall down, it did not take long for the Greeks to overcome the defenders and capture the city.

This incredible testimony was not only recorded by the victors, but by the defeated as well. Interestingly, while enemies most always never agree on anything, in this particular case, both armies corroborated each other's story.

Was this perhaps another "divine" intervention, or something else? Although Alexander himself did not subscribe to early Judean beliefs, incidentally the prophets Ezekiel and Isaiah had spoken of "God's curse" and the eventual destruction of the city of Tyre (Ezekiel, 27 & 28; Isaiah 23).

Who navigated the flying objects that helped Alexander to capture the city? Was this another unrecorded "divine" intervention in order for a prophecy to be fulfilled? Is this real history mixed with the divine, or did the gods of antiquity once more got involved in human interactions?

In either case, isn't it interesting that according to both modern and ancient religious accounts, "divine" powers seem to have always played a role in human affairs and ultimately helped fashion our history? Just like in the story of Sodom and Gomorrah, for example. Who were the angels that warned Lot and his family to flee, and what exactly was the mysterious "brimstone and fire" used to destroy these cities? Is it possible that this could be the same weapon described in the Indian epics?

Of course, just like with the Indian texts, the Old Testament is also full of similar stories of "flying vehicles," or "flying chariots" if you wish; and just like with the Indian accounts, all such depictions are either associated with angels—or God himself.

One notorious sighting of a flying machine was actually depicted in vivid detail by the prophet Ezekiel. Although Ezekiel's vision, as described in the Old Testament, is considered by theologians as the most vivid depiction of God, under a closer examination, it seems that the flying craft he witnessed, may have been similar in appearance to those described in Mahabharata during the same period.

In a primitive but very descriptive way, considering Ezekiel's technological limitations, he is giving us an extremely detailed account of a bright, round, metallic flying object that resembled a multilevel flying craft. According to Ezekiel, the flying gleaming object suddenly came out of the north, and once near him, it hovered for few moments before it opened its landing gear and landed in a fiery and noisy descent.

Just like any person with primitive or no technological understanding of a flying mechanical device, he describes modern technology while often he confuses moving mechanical parts as living creatures or limbs.

> And I looked, and, behold, a whirlwind came out of
> the north, a great cloud, and a fire enfolding itself, and
> a brightness was about it, and out of the midst thereof
> as the color of amber, out of the midst of the fire… also
> from within it came the likeness of four living creatures.
> [37] (Ezekiel 1:4–5.)

He describes a highly polished, circular object, made out of circular—or better yet, disc-shaped—compartments stacked up over each other. These circular decks that appeared to him as several different-size wheels, as he called them, they must have been stacked up on top of each other giving him the impression that each round compartment or *wheel* for lack of a better word, was progressively rising smaller, and in essence could fit into each other.

> And their appearance and their work was as it were a
> wheel within a wheel. [38] (Ezekiel 1:16.)

He further describes that the size and the height of the craft's round compartments, or the width of the rings, as he called them, were sizable and impressive.

> As for their rings, they were high and they were dread-
> ful; [39] (Ezekiel 1:18.)

Furthermore, he notices that one or more of the circular decks had what appeared to be windows or bright lights all around:

> And they four had their rings full of eyes round about.
> [40] (Ezekiel 1:18.)

According to his description, this metallic object descended near him after it first deployed its four polished landing gear posts.

> And they sparkled like the color of burnished brass...
> And their feet were straight feet; and the sole of their
> feet was like the sole of a calf's foot. [41] (Ezekiel 1:7.)

In his best analysis, as moving mechanical parts and robotic arms had to be alive in order to possess motion, it seems that the best way he could describe the extended arms of the landing gear under the center of the craft, it was that they resembled four living creatures:

> And out of the midst thereof came the likeness of four
> living creatures. [42] (Ezekiel 1:5.)

In closer observation though, he realized that the "power" of the craft did not rest in the landing gear, but it was within the craft's round fuselage compartments. He further tried to clarify that the landing gear was, in effect, stationary against the craft, and it moved in conjunction with the flying object.

> For the spirit of the living creature was in the wheels. When those went, these went, and when those stood, these stood; and when those were lifted up from the earth, the wheels were lifted up beside them. [43] (Ezekiel 1:21.)

On top of the craft, he noticed that there was a "crystal dome" that radiated a strong light from within... and inside the glass dome, he noticed a human figure.

> And over the heads of the living creatures there was the likeness of a firmament, like the color of the terrible ice, stretched forth over their heads above... And I saw as the color of electrum, as the appearance of fire round about enclosing it, from the appearance of his loins and upward... a figure with the appearance of a man. [44] (Ezekiel 1:22–27.)

Around the landing gear, as one would expect today, there were cover panels that once opened allowed for the landing gear to descend. As it was unimaginable to him to be able to fly without wings, as soon as the four landing gear panels opened, he assumed that those were the wings of the four creatures that descended. Of course, he also noticed that the opened panels below the craft and overhead the landing gear, never flapped once opened.

> And their wings touched they did not when they moved. [45] (Ezekiel 1:9.)

It is extremely fascinating that Ezekiel, in his primitive under-standing of technology, had sensed that this was ultimately a self-moving craft, emanating its own power for flight from within.

For the wind of the creature was in the wheels. [46]
(Ezekiel 1:20.)

He finally describes what could be either the craft's exhaust or propulsion system… as well as the sound that the craft made as it landed.

And from the appearance of his loins and downward
I saw as it were the appearance of fire, and there was
brightness round about him… I heard the noise of their
wings like the noise of great waters. [47] (Ezekiel 1:27.)

Although Ezekiel's description is certainly the most vivid close encounter with the "God" kind, there are several more descriptions in the Bible that point to alien (or God, if you wish) encounters.

For example, Enoch and Elijah were taken up by God while still alive. In fact, in a long list of genealogy where everyone else showed as deceased, Enoch remained alive because God took him.

And Enoch walked with God: and he disappeared from
the earth; for God took him. [48] (Genesis 5:24.)

In the case of Elijah, in a bit more dramatic way, God took him alive in a "fiery" (shiny) chariot by a "whirlwind."

And it came to pass, when the Lord would take up
Elijah into heaven by a whirlwind, that Elijah went
with Elisha from Gilgal… and it came to pass, as they
still went on, and talked, that, behold, there appeared
a chariot of fire, and horses of fire, and separated them;
and Elijah went up by a whirlwind into heaven. [49] (2
Kings 2:1–11.)

Is it possible that Elijah's fiery chariot was a flying machine like the one described by Ezekiel and similar to those of the Hindu scriptures? Certainly, the account of a bright flying object that landed in a fiery descent and lifted off in a "whirlwind" describes more of a physical event rather than a spiritual one. So while most theologians proclaim that such UFO descriptions are only figurative, a question remains: Why is there a need to attach a physical description in particular "spiritual" acts? Is it possible to assume that the authors of these stories manufactured the physical evidence, or could it be that due to their limited point of reference, they compared these flying machines to chariots and their occupants to angels or deities? Let's not forget that the word *chariot* in those days represented all means of transportation, while the word *heaven* meant the sky and not a unique place of reward after death.

# UFOS: PAST AND PRESENT

*Before the End of This Century, We will Make Contact
-- Prehistoric Cave carvings of UFO's -- UFO's in Religious
Art -- UFO Encounter: 74BC, Phrygia, Roman Republic
-- UFO Encounter: 1948, Capt. Thomas Mantell Incident
-- UFO Encounter: 1986, Japn Airlines – Flight 1628
-- UFO Encounter: 1987, Alaska Airlines – Flight 53
-- UFO Encounter: 1995, American West – Flight 564
-- UFO Encounter: 2006, Chicago O'Hare Airport
-- UFO Encounter: 1997, The Phoenix Lights -- UFO
Encounter: 1980, The Rendlesham Forest Incident*

Today, while 15 million people claim they have witnessed an unidenti-fied flying object, when asked, nearly half the population of our planet believes in the existence of extraterrestrials and/or UFOs. And why not! While considering that there are 100 billion stars just in our galaxy alone, each with their own planetary system, and with a universe that holds at least 100 billion galaxies, is it inconceivable to assume that other planets out there hold life? Metrodorus of Chios could not have used a better analogy 2,500 years ago:

> To suppose that Earth is the only populated world in infinite space, is as absurd as to believe that in an entire field sown with millet, only one grain will grow. [50]

So if we accept for a moment that alien life and consequently other extraterrestrial civilizations exist in other planets, is it possible then to assume that any of these civilizations could be thousands of years more advanced than our own? Of course we can! While our own solar system, at 4.6 billion years of age, is considered to be one of the newest "neighborhoods" in our own galaxy, and there are galaxies out there much older than our own galaxy by billions of years, isn't it logical to assume that life may have existed elsewhere before here on Earth? And following on the same hypothesis, as life elsewhere may be thousands, if not millions of years more advanced, isn't it possible that several of those civilizations could have evolved technologically enough for interstellar travel? Absolutely!

Often enough, classroom discussions about extraterrestrial intelligent life begin with an introduction to the Drake Equation. The famous equation was developed by Frank Drake in 1961 in order to codify all the important factors that, once multiplied, could determine how many intelligent civilizations could be in our galaxy.

The amazing thing about the Drake Equation is that no matter how conservative you are with the values of the individual factors, it leads to an incredibly large number of ETs out there, with technology and radios, attempting to contact one another.

## The Drake Equation [51]
$$N = R_* \, f_p \, n_e \, f_l \, f_i \, f_c \, L$$

Where:

$R_*$ is the total number of stars in the Milky Way galaxy.

$f_p$ is the fraction of stars that have planets around them.

$n_e$ is the number of planets per star that are capable of sustaining life.

$f_l$ is the fraction of planets in $n_e$ where life evolves.

$f_i$ is the fraction of $f_l$ where intelligent life evolves.

$f_c$ is the fraction of $f_i$ that communicate.

**L** is fraction of the planet's life during which the communicating civilizations live and attempt contact.

**N**, the resulting product, is the total number of communicating civilizations in the galaxy.

Dr. Michio Kaku, a renowned physicist, predicted, in a speech given to Global Competitiveness Forum in Saudi Arabia in 2011 with the title "Contact: Learning from Outer Space," that some time before the middle of this century, we may eventually come in contact with another civilization in outer space—one that could be thousands, or even millions of years more technologically advanced than our own.

In his speech, he further explained that when physicists are looking for advanced civilizations in space, they don't look for "little green men" as he put it, but for energy consumption. He also explained that there are three types of advanced civilizations in space: type-1, type-2, and type-3 civilizations.

He explained that a type-1 civilization has the power of an entire planet. This civilization can control the weather, mine the oceans, and has the potential to control earthquakes and volcanoes. This civilization is called a planetary civilization.

A type-2 civilization in space has the power to control the output of a star. Nothing known to science, he explained, can destroy a type-2 civilization. They can modify ice ages, deflect meteors, and even the death of their sun is not a problem to a type-2 civilization. Technologically, they are capable enough to move their planet, reignite their star or even find a new star in space. This is called a stellar civilization.

A type-3 civilization is known as a galactic civilization. A type-3 civilization can manage the energy that makes space unstable. It is possible for a type-3 civilization to control gateways, wormholes, and portholes—perhaps to other dimensions. According to Dr. Kaku, a type-3 civilization is so powerful it can ultimately alter the fabric of space and time.

Interestingly, at the end of his speech, when Dr. Kaku compared us to the above scale, he labeled Earth as a type-0 civilization. He did predict, though, that once we are able to surpass certain theological implications, and continue to advance technologically, by the beginning of the 22nd century, we will eventually become a type-1 civilization.

Of course, the question remains. Even as a type-1 civilization could we ever compete with a type-2 or a type-3 civilization if we ever came in contact with one? As it appears, according to Dr. Kaku, that would be absolutely impossible as clearly new laws of physics "open up" for type-2 and type-3 civilizations.

Is it possible then to assume that while these civilizations possess power and technologies beyond our modern understanding, if any one of them made it here on Earth, during our prehistory, could we have misinterpreted them as gods and their technology as divine power? Of course it's possible! In fact, this is the premise of every religion, that not only humans were created by another "supreme being"; but throughout our evolution and during our history, it seems we have always been "guided" by celestial gods.

Even though many people today tend to see the UFO phenomenon as an invention of the 20th century, we must remind ourselves that a great number of UFO sightings were not reported in modern times during the evening news; but such reports, or better yet depictions of UFOs can be found all over the world—in prehistoric caves, as well as in religious art. It seems that from the beginning of time, humans noticed and illustrated such encounters of unidentified flying objects. In truth, there is so much documentation of UFOs in cave carvings and religious art, is hard to believe that more people are not aware of these depictions? Are we so well-conditioned that still we don't see Mary Magdalene seated next to Jesus in the famous Leonardo da Vinci's painting of the Last Supper? Even with our modern awareness of technology, it seems that we still choose to consider that a spiritual entity, like God, occasionally assumes a physical form and uses mechanical means of transportation rather than considering the alternative.

Of course, when it comes to religious art or cave depictions of UFOs, it goes without saying, the majority of anthropologists who are not-so-fond of controversy quickly explain that those are the symbols of the sun and the moon. Some experts (and most people), though, are clearly puzzled by many of these depictions, as the objects portrayed are unlike anything thought to have existed in the caveman's natural environment. Some objects actually appear to be symmetrical, aerodynamic in design, and in some cases have a modern-day technological look to them. If those are not depictions of UFOs, we must admit that they look a great deal like the sketches observers draw today, regarding their own encounters with UFOs.

When observing and comparing these shapes to modern illustrations, not only do they appear to look the same, but it becomes clear that these sightings had the same profound impact on the ancient artists who considered them significant enough to decorate their cave walls with.

The explanation by skeptics that these objects figuratively represent the sun and the moon, and the fact they appear in many other cave depictions around the world, does not prove that these objects illustrate regular celestial bodies in the sky. Skeptics cannot explain this phenomenon away by presenting more evidence that support it.

Actually, UFOs are not only depicted in caves by prehistoric men. Incredibly enough, Christian art also contains several of these "unexplained" illustrations! Among many such depictions, a good example is one called, *The Madonna with Saint Giovannino*, a 15th century painting. What is interesting about this religious depiction is that directly behind the left shoulder of Madonna, on a cliff and far in the background, is the image of a man with his dog looking upward toward what appears to be a gleaming UFO in the sky. In fact, in order to get a better glimpse, the man has his right palm over his eyes as if he is trying to get a good look at the object!

While critics, once again, claim that the flying objects in these depictions represent none other than the moon and the sun, it is obvious that this is not the case—as in various other religious paintings, the moon and sun are normally depicted. If anything, it becomes apparent that the unidentified flying objects had the same effect on the people during the Renaissance as they did on people during our prehistory.

*The Madonna with Saint Giovannino (a 15th century painting by Domenico Ghirlandaio). In the background, over her left shoulder (right top corner), a man and his dog are observing a flying object.*

Is it possible then to assume that due to limited technological reference, to explain such sightings during the Renaissance, religious scholars and the early church associated such sightings with the divine, and artists who often were hired to depict divine acts were allowed to incorporate these "symbols of divinity" into their paintings? And if these objects are simply figurative as some skeptics argue, why the clear need to portray those alongside the image of Christ, for instance? Why did religious artists create such an abomination, and most importantly, why did the church allow such pagan symbols to exist alongside its holy figures?

The fact that they kept on repeating these depictions from one century to another, rather than eliminating such symbols altogether, further reinforces the suspicion that the objects in these paintings were actually physical objects of past unexplained encounters. It also appears that, for the same reason the early church accepted the Old Testament in its entirety, although often it severely contradicted the New Testament and the teachings of Christ, for the same reason they allowed for the adaptation of these flying objects in religious depictions as these "symbols" always in the past represented the "divine."

Slowly, slowly though, the modern Church transforms. While many of these questions and "mysteries" still go unanswered, in November of 2009 and to everyone's surprise, (considering the past position of the Church on the existence of other alien civilizations), the Vatican finally conceded that extraterrestrial life is possible and that its presence does not contradict with the beliefs of the Church.

When until now, the UFO phenomenon and other claims of extraterrestrial life were viewed with high skepticism, or even ridicule, this surprising and official proclamation by the Catholic Church helps to bring UFOs and the possibility of extraterrestrial life forward, and thus as an acceptable topic, further closer to mainstream science. The ultimate question remains to be answered though: Are UFOs extraterrestrial? Are they a figment of peoples' imagination, or secret military projects? Could it be all of the above? Actually, most experts today who study cases of UFOs agree that out of all reported sightings, five percent of those defy any explanation, and remain a mystery.

Such, without a doubt, are several sightings reported prior to the 1900s and before the invention of flight!

One such documented UFO encounter was recorded in 74 BC in Phrygia, Asia, which at the time was a Roman Republic territory. According to Plutarch, a Roman army commanded by Lucullus was about to engage in a battle with Mithridates VI of Pontus, when suddenly, "the sky burst open and a huge 'flamelike' body was seen to land between the two armies." According to Plutarch, the shiny object resembled a "wine jar" and had a "molten silver" color. The apparently highly polished, silvery object was reported by both armies.

Just after the invention of flight by the Wright Brothers in 1909, mystery airships, strange moving lights, and some solid objects in the sky were seen around Otago and elsewhere in New Zealand and were reported to newspapers.

In more modern times, on January 7, 1948, dozens of residents of the Madisonville, Kentucky, area called the police to report a large circular object hovering in the sky, giving off a brilliant glow. The state police alerted Air Force officials at Goodman Field, an airbase located at Fort Knox. About 15 minutes later, the airfield's tower spotted the UFO as well and radioed a squadron of P-51 fighters already aloft to further investigate.

The squadron leader Captain Thomas Mantell Jr., an expert pilot who had won the Distinguished Flying Cross for bravery during World War 2, responded that he had also noticed the UFO and was in pursuit. Three minutes later, Mantell's plane crashed, killing its pilot. Just before the crash, Manttell was quoted saying,

> "I am closing in now to take a good look… this thing looks metallic and is tremendous in size." [52]

After an investigation, the official conclusion was that Captain Mantell had run out of oxygen and crashed during the pursuit.

More recently, one of the most famous modern-day reports of a UFO encounter is that of Japan Airlines – Flight 1628.

This incident occurred on November 17, 1986, and involved a Japanese cargo jumbo freighter aircraft en route from Paris to Narita, Tokyo. In the cockpit was Captain Kenju Terauchi, an ex-fighter pilot with more than 10,000 hours of flight experience. Also in the cockpit were the co-pilot, Takanori Tamefuji, and flight engineer, Yoshio Tsukuba.

Between Reykjavik and Anchorage, over eastern Alaska, at 5:11 p.m., and at an altitude of 35,000 feet, the crew first witnessed two unidentified objects to their left, roughly 2,000 feet below their altitude. The two objects appeared to be following on the same path and speed. At about 5:18 p.m., the two crafts abruptly rose from below and closed in to accompany the aircraft. They veered to a position of about 500 feet from the airliner. According to the crew, each had two rectangular arrays of what appeared to be glowing nozzles or thrusters, though their bodies remained obscured by the darkness of night. The crew also reported that, at times, the two objects were flying so close that the aircraft's cabin was lit up, and they could feel the radiating heat on their faces. More incredibly, though, the two objects not only appeared to be toying with the airliner, but throughout the entire encounter, they displayed what captain Terauchi later described as a disregard for inertia:

> The thing was flying as if there was no such thing as gravity. It sped up, then stopped, then flew at our speed, in our direction, so that to us it [appeared to be] standing still. The next instant it changed course.... In other words, the flying object had overcome gravity. [53]

For those not familiar with the term, *inertia* is the resistance of any physical object to a change in its state of motion or rest, or the tendency of an object to resist any change in its motion. The principle of inertia is one of the fundamental principles of classical physics, which is used to describe the motion of matter and how it is affected by applied forces.

At about 5:19 p.m., air traffic control was notified of the incident, although they could not confirm the objects in the indicated position. After three or four minutes, the two UFOs assumed side-by-side configuration, which they maintained for the next few minutes. According to Captain Terauchi, while in formation, they accompanied the aircraft with a rising and falling motion. Few more minutes later, the two objects left abruptly and moved below the horizon to the east.

Once the two objects disappeared, Captain Terauchi noticed a pale group of lights that matched their altitude and direction. After setting their onboard radarscope to a 25-nautical-mile (46 km) range, he confirmed another object ahead at about 7.5 miles (13.9 kilometers) and informed ATC of the object's presence.

As Fairbanks city lights began to illuminate the object, captain Terauchi identified the shape of a huge "spaceship" on his portside, "twice the size of an aircraft carrier," and he immediately requested a change of course to avoid it! The huge object, however, followed the airliner "in formation" throughout a 45 degree turn, a descent from 35,000 to 31,000 feet, and finally a 360-degree turn. Although the short-range radar at Fairbanks failed to register the object, the ATC offered military intervention, which reportedly was declined by the fighter pilot due to his knowledge of the Mantell incident!

Eventually, JAL 1628 lost sight of the large UFO and arrived safely in Anchorage at around 6:20 p.m.

On January 29, 1987, at 6:40 p.m., Alaska Airlines Flight 53 observed a fast moving object on their onboard radar. While traveling at 35,000 feet, about 60 miles (97 km) west of McGrath, on a flight from Nome to Anchorage, their radar registered an object in front of them, at about 25 miles (40 km) range. While they could not see the object or any light, visually they noticed that, on radar, the object was increasing its distance at a very high speed. With every sweep of their radar, 1 second apart, the object was traveling 5 miles, translating to a speed of 18,000 mph (29,000 km/h).

Interestingly enough, the very next day, a US Air Force KC-135 jet flying from Anchorage to Fairbanks once again observed a very large, disc-shaped object. The pilot reported that the object came as close as 12 meters (40 feet) from the aircraft! The object eventually disappeared out of sight.

On May 25, 1995, on a flight from Tampa, Florida, to Dallas and then to Las Vegas, just after 9:00 p.m., Flight 564 of America West reported they were followed by a cigar-shaped UFO. The Boeing 757 was flying over the Texas panhandle at 35,000 feet when first a flight attendant and then the rest of the crew noticed a row of lights below them somewhere between 30,000 and 35,000 feet. Background lightning allowed them occasionally to better see the image of the UFO, which later they described as a cigar-shaped object, 300-500 feet long, with a horizontal row of 8 strobe lights that flashed in sequence from left to right.

On November 7, 2006, at about 4:15 p.m., federal authorities received a report that several United Airline employees and pilots were witnessing a sighting of a saucer-shaped craft hovering over Chicago O'Hare Airport.

The object was first spotted by a ramp employee who was pushing back United Airlines Flight 446. Shortly after, several more airport employees and many more independent witnesses outside the airport noticed the object. Someone described it as a disc-shaped craft hovering over the airport's tower. According to the same witness, the nearby observers gasped as the object eventually shot through the clouds at high velocity, leaving a clear blue hole in the cloud layer.

According to an article that followed in the Chicago Tribune newspaper, "The disk was visible for approximately two minutes."

Another famous UFO encounter in the late '90s happened on March 13, 1997. It is recorded and remembered by many as the Phoenix Lights.

In this particular incident, thousands of eyewitnesses observed a huge carpenter's square-shaped UFO with five round lights or light-emitting engines. Fife Symington, the governor of Arizona at the time, who also witnessed the incident he later called the object otherworldly.

At 6:55 p.m., a man first reported seeing a V-shaped object above Henderson, Nevada. He said the craft was about the "size of a Boeing 747." It had six lights on its leading edge and sounded like "a rushing wind." He reported that the UFO was headed from northwest to southeast. A former police officer from Paulden, Arizona, was the next person to report the sighting after leaving his house at 8:15 p.m. A few minutes later, several phone calls began to come in, and callers reported a solid object that blocked out much of the starry sky as it passed overhead.

John Kaiser and his family were outside in Prescott Valley when they noticed a cluster of lights to their west-northwest. The lights formed a triangular pattern. About two to three minutes later, the object passed directly overhead and then disappeared in the night sky to the southeast of Prescott Valley. According to them and many other witnesses, the object was flying fairly low and made no sound whatsoever.

Tim Ley and his family also noticed the strange lights when they were above Prescott Valley and about 60 miles (100 kilometers) away from them. After about ten minutes or so, as the lights got closer, they could make out the shape of the object which looked like a 60-degree carpenter's square with five lights set into it. One light was at the front of the aircraft, and two were on each side. The object with the embedded lights, as they explained, silently flew over their neighborhood very low and so slowly that, at times, it appeared to hover. Eventually, the object flew toward the Squaw Peak Mountain and Phoenix Sky Harbor International Airport.

Witnesses in Glendale, a suburb northwest of Phoenix, also saw the object pass over their neighborhood at an altitude high enough to become obscured by the low clouds. This was at approximately between 8:30 and 8:45 p.m.

The following day, on March 14, 1997, four Phoenix men were reported missing in the Estrella Mountains. Glenn Lauder (28), Mitch Adams (29), Ryan Stone (27), and Jacob Reynolds (28), were all reported missing after they were last seen at the base of the Estrella mountain range, where the sightings took place.

It is worth to mention that the National UFO Reporting Center received the following report from the Prescott area:

> While doing astrophotography I observed five yellow-white lights in a V formation moving slowly from the northwest, across the sky to the northeast, then turn almost due south and continue until out of sight. The point of the V was in the direction of movement. The first three lights were in a fairly tight V while two of the lights were further back along the lines of the V's legs. During the NW-NE transit one of the trailing lights moved up and joined the three and then dropped back to the trailing position. I estimated the three light V to cover about 0.5 degrees of sky and the whole group of five lights to cover about 1 degree of sky. [54]

On June 18, 1997, after months of silence from the national media, *USA Today* carried an article on the front page of the newspaper with the headline: SKIES, PHONE LINES, LIGHT UP ARIZONA.

Journalist Richard Price wrote, "So far there is no explanation, but the government is not investigating. Local and federal agencies disagree over who should pursue the report…" Price also asserted that the events of March 13th "may add up to the most contentious and confounding UFO report since the so-called UFO age was launched 50 years ago by the legendary crash of a 'spaceship' outside Roswell, New Mexico."

Price listed three things in his article that witnesses generally agreed upon: (1) The object was enormous, with the most conservative estimate describing it as three football fields long (although computer analysis of the tapes showed the object to be 6000 feet and more than a mile wide); (2) it made no sound; and (3) it cruised over Phoenix at 30 mph and hovered in place several times in the sky.

In his article, Price also mentioned that although the air traffic controllers could see the lights of the UFO, they could not assist pilots in the area as their radar screens did not register the object. Price also shared words about the incident with many eyewitnesses, including a 31 year-old laser printer technician, Dana Valentine. Valentine was in his yard when he noticed the lights. Soon after, he and his father, an aeronautics engineer, both observed the object flying directly above them at an altitude of about 500 feet. Valentine said, "We could see the outline of a mass behind the lights, but you couldn't actually see the mass. It was like a grey distortion of the night sky, wavy. I don't know exactly what it was, but I know it's not a technology the public has heard before." Price also wrote that, according to Jim Dilettoso and Michael Tanner, "Neither has anybody else!"

Michael and Jim are two out of four partners who own Village Labs, a Tempe, Arizona, company that designs supercomputers for the federal government as well as computerized special effects for Hollywood. Occasionally, they also moonlight as analysts of UFO tapes. According to Michael and Jim, the lights over Phoenix were dramatically unique. Each was "a perfect, uniform light, with no variation from one edge to the other, and no glow." After seeing the tapes, they ruled out aircraft lights, flares, holograms, and lasers as sources of the lights.

The Rendlesham Forest Incident is the name given to a series of sightings of unexplained lights, and the landing of a UFO in Rendlesham Forest, Suffolk, England, during the last week of December in 1980. The incident happened just outside RAF Woodbridge and near RAF Bendwaters, two military bases used at the time by the U.S. Air Force.

Dozens of base personnel witnessed the various events taking place over a two- to three-day period.

The bases are located about 8 miles (13 km) east of the town of Ipswich. The forest bordering those consists of about 6 square miles (15 square kilometers) of coniferous and broadleaf trees. At the time of the incident, both bases were under the command of wing commander Col. Gordon E. Williams. The base commander was Col. Ted Conrad, and the deputy commander was Lt. Col. Charles I. Halt. What is most intriguing about this incident is that, Lt. Col. Halt personally witnessed the encounter and immediately after the incident, he forwarded a memo of the event to the Ministry of Defense.

The main events of the incident, including the alleged landing described by one of the servicemen, took place in the forest and near the east gate of RAF Woodbridge, where night guards first noticed mysterious lights descending into the forest. The forest at that location extends east about one mile (1.6 kilometers) beyond the east gate and ends at a farmer's field.

On December 27, 1980, at around 3:00 a.m., strange lights were spotted by a security patrol near the east gate of RAF Woodbridge. Although servicemen thought initially that the lights belonged to a downed aircraft, upon entering the forest to investigate, they saw a small glowing object, metallic in appearance, with colored lights. As they approached, the object began to move through the trees. The servicemen also noticed that the craft had left three depressions on the ground where it had landed.

Later, Sgt. Jim Penniston, one of the servicemen first to arrive at the scene, also claimed that he came in contact with the unidentified object. He claimed to have touched its warm surface, he witnessed its triangular landing gear and took detailed notes of its features and of the numerous symbols on its body. According to Sgt. Penniston, the object lifted from the ground and in absolute silence flew away after the brief encounter.

On the morning of December 27, when servicemen returned to the site, they found the three impressions left behind by the craft and plaster casts of the imprints were taken.

On the following evening, as the strange lights reappeared, several servicemen along with Lt. Col. Halt returned to the site and in the early hours of December 29, with radiation measuring devices and detected radiation in the three depressions left behind by the UFO. Deputy base commander Lt. Col. Halt recorded the events on a micro-cassette recorder.

Lieutenant Colonel Halt reported that later in the night, a red sunlike light was seen through the trees. It moved around, pulsed, and at one point it appeared to "throw off" glowing particles. Suddenly, the strange light broke into five separate white objects and then all of them disappeared. Immediately after, three starlike objects were noticed in the sky, two to the north, and one to the south, about 10 degrees above the horizon. According to Lt. Col. Halt, two of the objects moved rapidly in sharp angular movements and when got closer displayed red, green, and blue lights. The object to the south remained in the sky for a long time and beamed down a stream of light from time to time.

The incident was originally published in the tabloid paper *News of the World*, on October 2, 1983, under the headline: UFO Lands in Suffolk – and That's Official. The initial story was based on an account given by a former U.S. airman, Larry Warren, under the fake name of Art Wallace. The first piece of primary evidence to be made public was the memorandum written by the deputy base commander, Lt. Col. Halt, to the Ministry of Defense. Known as the Halt Memo, this was made available first in the United States under the U.S. Freedom of Information Act in 1983. The memo was dated January 13, 1981, and it was titled "Unexplained Lights."

Several years later, on June 2010, retired Lt. Col. Charles I. Halt in a notarized affidavit once again summarized what had happened, and he repeated that he believed the event to be extraterrestrial. He also reiterated that both, the United States and United Kingdom had covered up the incident:

> I believe the objects that I saw at close quarter were extraterrestrial in origin and that the security services of both the United States and the United Kingdom have attempted—both then and now—to subvert the significance of what occurred at Rendlesham Forest and RAF Bentwaters by the use of well-practiced methods of disinformation. [55]

In the same affidavit, Halt also dismissed past claims that he and his men had confused the lighthouse light with a UFO.

> While in Rendlesham Forest, our security team observed a light that looked like a large eye, red in color, moving through the trees. After a few minutes, this object began dripping something that looked like molten metal. A short while later it broke into several smaller, white-colored objects which flew away in all directions. Claims by skeptics that this was merely a sweeping beam from a distant lighthouse are unfounded; we could see the unknown light and the lighthouse simultaneously. The latter was 35 to 40-degrees off where all of this was happening. [56]

The late Lord Hill-Norton, admiral of the fleet and former chief of the U.K. Defense Staff, also believed that a UFO had landed at Rendlesham and repeatedly questioned the U.K. government on the issue. He argued that an incident like this at a nuclear weapons base was of national security interest.

Answering his inquiry, Baroness Symons of Vernham Dean replied, "Special Branch officers may have been aware of the incident but would not have shown any interest unless there was evidence of a potential threat to national security. No such interest appears to have been shown."

This answer obviously did not satisfy Lord Hill-Norton, as he later replied, "Either large numbers of people were hallucinating, and for an American Air Force nuclear base this is extremely dangerous, or what they say happened did happen, and in either of those circumstances there can only be one answer and that is of extreme defense interest."

Of course, while the above cases as with all UFO reports are being denied by the United States Government, behind the scenes the U.S. military, as well as the first responders in United States, properly are training for the possibility of an extraterrestrial encounter. If the official position is that UFO's and ETs "do not exist," why the training exercises? For instance, fire departments around the country utilize a training manual (*Fire Officer's Guide to Disaster Control, Second Edition, Chapter 13, under the title "Enemy Attack and UFO Potential"*) which not only introduces cases of past UFO encounters, but explicitly advises the first responders on how to act in the event of a downed UFO or injured extraterrestrials. If the fire officer's training is solely "for the perceived existence (of UFO's) which creates the potential for panic, injury and even death," why the detailed reference of past UFO encounters, and the apparent instructions in the department's manual on how to literally deal with alien crafts or extraterrestrial beings? How can specific instructions on how to deal with a downed UFO and injured extraterrestrials provide preparedness on how to handle public hysteria, unless, of course, the chapter is there to prepare the department for the inevitable, as well as to provide basic training on how to quarantine an area until the proper authorities arrive?

# OUR MYSTERIOUS PAST

*The Baffling Nazca Lines -- The Alien-Looking
Elongated Skulls of Antiquity -- The Mysterious King
Akhenaten -- Did "Angels" Procreate with Humans?
-- The Zuni Tribe and Sirius Mystery -- Huang Di:
Mysteries of the "Yellow Emperor" -- The Dropa Discs*

All around the world, there are many ancient sites that even today, after years of study, still remain shrouded in mystery.

Such is the site of the Nazca Lines in Peru. The site, located in Nazca, Peru—hence its name—is one of the most enigmatic places in the world. Not for its megalithic structures, but for the mysterious 2000 year-old earth carvings the Nazca people left behind in a desolated area that covers more than 500 square miles. Here, etched on the ground, there are hundreds of lines, geometric shapes, and images of animals and birds. Some lines are straight and remain perfectly straight for several miles, while others loop around and seem to go nowhere. Oddly enough, some etchings even look like modern day airstrips.

Although these geoglyphs were done by only removing the loose surface stone and lightly carving shapes into the ground, the weather elements in this area are such that the Nazca site today looks nearly as it did two thousand years ago. It is an odd site that had baffled many researchers over the last fifty years.

According to mainstream historians, the images here were created by the Nazca Indians, who flourished in this area from around 200 BC to around 600 AD. Graves and other ruins found nearby also lead to speculations that this may have been a religious site.

The mysterious Nazca lines were spotted for the first time by pilots during the late 1920s as they were reporting strange lines and what appeared to be landing strips in the middle of nowhere.

By the way, it is important to mention that these earth illustrations are nearly invisible to the naked eye while on the ground. As the Nazca images lack 3-dimensional structure, unlike the crop circles where the corn or wheat extends few feet above the ground, these lines or designs are flat to the ground and ultimately disappear into the surface of the landscape that is also heavily covered with scattered stone. Indeed, while at first look, Nazca appears to be just another desolated area, the entire site comes alive with images when looked upon from the air. Without a doubt, it is an impressive site. To think how much time and effort the Nazca people invested in filling up this enormous area with images is mind-boggling.

What prompted these otherwise primitive people to use the landscape here as a gigantic canvas? Why so much effort was put into something that, once completed, it could never be seen or recognized again by another human being? Why these illustrations were made so large that they only could be seen from a high altitude? Whose attention were they trying to catch, and how high did they mean for these images to project? And finally, what really motivated the Nazca people to keep coming back to draw more and more illustrations?

Actually there are so many images and lines here that several depictions overlap each other. This is a clear sign that even the Nazca Indians themselves, once they finished an etching, could not clearly identify its location, thus often newer etchings ended up overlapping older ones. Once again, why so many images, and what was their message?

When "sifting" through the plethora of images though, it becomes unquestionably clear that the most intriguing image on the whole site is the outline of a "standing man," later nicknamed the "astronaut." Like the rest of the illustrations, this figure is so large it covers an entire hill site.

What is so interesting about this image is the man's posture. The man is depicted upright with his left arm held straight down while his right hand is raised as if he "greets" someone up in the sky. It is as if the creators of the "astronaut" brilliantly recognized that although not everyone can read or interpret geometric images, signs, or understand a foreign language, everyone from this world and beyond, can understand this man's posture and body language. Without a doubt, this is typical posture of a man with friendly intentions and the raised hand is a gesture of goodwill. Of course, since these images were not meant to be recognizable from the ground, for whom exactly was this friendly message intended for? Was it for the "gods" perhaps?

Those who may not quite see the symbolism in that image should be reminded of the following:

In 1972, Pioneer 10 and later in 1973, Pioneer 11 spacecrafts were the first human-built objects designed to leave our solar system. Two plaques were especially created for the two crafts, and they were attached to their antenna support struts in such a way that they would be visible, but also be protected from stellar dust that could ultimately damage them.

Both plaques featured the nude figures of a man and a woman along with several symbols that were designed to provide information about the origin of the spacecraft. Along with a unique disc that plays verbal messages, music, and sounds from planet Earth, the two plaques were created by NASA with the sole purpose of relaying a visual communication to any extraterrestrial that could intercept any of the two spacecrafts during their long journey.

What was so compelling about NASA's message though, is that the standing man on the spacecraft's plaque has his left arm straight down while his right hand is raised as a symbol of "goodwill." Not surprisingly, modern scientists decided that this was the very best way to visually communicate our friendly intentions to another extraterrestrial race. NASA depicted exactly the same posture and gesture the primitive Indians picked in order to relay their intentions to those who could fly overhead and witness their image.

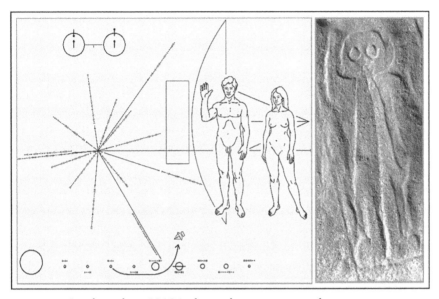

*On the right, a NASA plaque depicts a man and a woman, among other things. The man's right hand is raised as a gesture of good will and friendship. This plaque was originally mouunted by NASA in both Pioneer 10 & 11 spacecrafts (1972 & 1973) in the event they were intercepted by an extraterrestrial life. The image on the right which is 1200 feet long and can only be seen from a high altitude, was carved on the ground in the Nazca Desert by the Nazca culture more than 2000 years ago.*

So to whom were these images directed? Were the symbols meant to be for some imaginary gods the Nazca people invented in need of worship, or were they meant for real flesh and blood "gods" that the Indians came in contact with? Judging by the monumental work that took place at the Nazca plateau, they must have witnessed something very profound in order to employ such a feat and continue this tradition for centuries.

The graves found in the immediate area, of course, hint on the hypothesis that this site may have been a spiritual place. But who or what gave the Nazca people the divine inspiration about this particular desolated area? And if this was a "holy ground," what did all the lines mean? Is it possible to assume that the images were religious offerings, or perhaps visual contributions to the "gods"? Let's not forget that this is a tradition that is practiced by every civilization from the beginning of time. The ancient Egyptians did it by building megalithic structures. In modern times, people tend to make similar offerings and ultimately build churches, sculptures, or even offer religious paintings when God grants their wishes. Actually, the fact that several lines and shapes at Nazca overlap each other further confirms the likelihood that each etching, or offering, was done by a different group of people, at a different time, and with no clear idea where the previous etchings were located.

But why did these "gods" visit Nazca to begin with? What could an extraterrestrial race possibly want from a desolated area like Nazca? Before answering though, we must first ask ourselves why we are making plans to colonize the Moon and eventually Mars. As inhospitable as these places are (obviously much worse than Nazca), what could be our motive behind such plans? The answer is obviously precious metals and minerals, of course.

If ETs landed at Nazca (and suspiciously some clues point that they did), who created the huge animal geoglyphs and geometric symbols here? Is it possible that the Nazca gods helped create some of these designs as some UFOlogists suggest? Most likely they did not. If anything, it seems that the Nazca people could have made those by themselves. Just like the crop circles that can be done by few skilled people, there is no doubt that the local Indians could have done all these geoglyphs. It is no easy task, as some researchers already demonstrated, but is totally achievable.

So if the etchings were done by the local Indians, are there other clues on this site that could suggest the presence of someone else more technologically advanced? The answer, actually, is yes! In fact, under closer observation, some lines at the Nazca site suspiciously resemble vehicle tracks! These tire tracks, for lack of a better word, a pair of lines that sit perfectly parallel to each other and traverse the landscape from point A to point B, forming no particular design—they provide the first clue. The second, and by far, most important clue, comes from a particular monumental landscape modification nearby that seems to be the work of someone who was properly equipped with heavy machinery!

Just slightly north of Nazca, there is the tiny town of Palpa. Mixed in the mountainous landscape around Palpa, there is a mountain range that was artificially flattened. Actually, the fact that all the other hills and mountains in the area have their peaks and ridges intact makes this anomaly even more obvious.

When looking at this bizarre site for the first time, not only it appears as if someone "shaved" the entire mountain range, but it looks as if they did it without leaving behind any debris. Of course, under a closer examination, it becomes more evident that the debris was pushed to the sides, thus enlarging the massive landing strip that now appears to dominate this mountainous platform. This special mountaintop not only points to an immense project that the local tribes could not have done on their own with picks and shovels, but also provides a clue as to why the mysterious lines at Nazca and the surrounding area may have gotten started in the first place.

Of course, while it is not quite clear why anyone would choose to "shave" this particular mountaintop over another, once flattened, the shaved mountain became a perfect "stage area." The huge artificial platform provides a theater of operations in a safe elevated position and a place where lots of material can be stored over time.

Out of all places, though, why would an ET select Nazca? Once again, the answer must be natural resources. We know today that Nazca and the surrounding area hold an enormous wealth of various metals and minerals. In a short distance, and just south of the Nazca site, the Marcona mine holds the largest known iron oxide (+/- copper-gold) deposits in the Pacific coastal belt of South America. Presently, mining is also the central element in Peru's economy. The Andes are also rich in minerals and gold. Although Peru ranks eighth worldwide in gold production, it ranks first in Latin America. It ranks second in copper worldwide and is one of the five top producers of lead and zinc.

What provoked Nazca to become a religious place, though, and why the ceremonial line-making that followed? Is it possible that the sight of the flattened mountain range nearby and the machine-made tracks left behind by the "gods" sparked the crazy obsession of the line-making? Certainly, while anything created by the "gods" could have been worshiped as a divine characteristic, even mimicking machine tracks was a practice that could have connected the Nazca to their deities. As for the etchings that resemble airstrips, those perhaps were created to mimic the landing strip seen on the mountainous platform near Palpa.

Of course, after the "gods" departed, the line-making was eventually replaced with various other shapes, including animal outlines that the locals were more accustomed to.

If ETs landed at Nazca for metal exploration though (as in the case of South Africa), should there be some secret messages or mathematical codes associated with their landing, as some UFOlogists suggest some of the Nazca lines represent? Of course not! Extraterrestrials would not care to leave messages for future human generations. On the other hand, if they were exploring or mining the area around Nazca, more machine-made remnants should have been left behind. Actually, they are! Essentially, the flattened mountain near Palpa is not the only site that supports the use of heavy equipment. Another enigmatic site nearby, nicknamed the Band of Holes, further supports that possibility.

This site is located about 150 kilometers north of Nazca and just about 50 kilometers east of San Clemente. It is another site shrouded in mystery and one that puzzled mainstream archaeologists for decades. In fact, no one to this day knows who made it, or why. The Band of Holes site is just couple of kilometers east of the tiny village of Humay and just off Route 26. It is an artificial site so vast that one can best appreciate it from the air.

Just as its name insinuates, it consists of thousands of holes on the ground that form a band approximately 24 meters wide and about 2 kilometers long. Each hole measures about 1 meter in diameter and has a depth of more than one meter. There are 8 holes across to make the width of the band, and they appear to be climbing the hillside in a repetitive uniformed fashion as they roll over the rocky mountainous terrain until they abruptly end in what it seems to be the remnants of an oval-shaped crater.

Mainstream archaeologists originally suggested that these holes were made to store grains, but once that theory was proven wrong, they suggested that these could be personal tombs. As before with the grain theory, nothing was ever found here to suggest that this could have been a burial site. On the other hand, the holes appear to have been made by a massive drilling rig that methodically climbed up the hill testing the geology of the site. In fact, the shallow crater at the end of the band should be further examined in order to determine if any mining took place there more than 2,000 years ago.

How long the ETs mined Nazca, and/or whether this was even a successful mining site for them is not known. What seems to be certain though is that while here, most likely they came in contact with the local population that regarded them as divine beings. How do we know that? How else do we explain the taboo of skull deformation among the Nazca people, if not to mimic another "divine" form? Strangely enough, several skeleton remains found near Nazca had some "alien-looking" elongated skulls. The excavation of several graves at this site actually helped archaeologists to recognize that skull deformation was not always a common practice among the Nazca people, but a tradition that started at some particular point in their history. Before that time, skeletal remains were found to have normal skulls.

Interestingly, while it is widely known by historians that the Nazca people worshiped various nature gods—like the killer whale, the harvesters, the serpentine creature, and others—the most prevalent of all worshiped figures in their culture was an "anthropomorphic" being. Who was this divine being and what he looked like is anyone's guess. Is it possible to assume that these anthropomorphic beings had elongated heads and ultimately were the reason behind the Nazca head deformation?

Like with the Indian obsession to mimic the "lines" of the "gods," is it possible that the skull deformation started in order to mimic the image of the "gods?" What else could have triggered their desire to begin implying such inhumane measures on the skulls of their children in order to achieve such results?

In 1870, in the African Congo, we discovered that yet another tribe was practicing this same bizarre deformation. Since childbirth, parents tied and forced their children's skulls to deform and to become elongated.

Ultimately, few more cultures around the world, totally unknown to each other, and even on different continents, were found to have practiced the same head deformation. Why though? What possibly could have triggered this practice? What motivated certain people around the planet to begin such rituals and to inflict such cruel practices on themselves? Was this simply a rare and bizarre coincidence they invented on their own, or was it done to resemble their "gods," as some claim? Certainly something profound must have happened in order for this bizarre concept to have taken place.

Some of the most compelling cases of elongated skulls actually can be traced back to ancient Egypt. This was a period where the Egyptian faith, under King Akhenaten (1353 BC), talked about a time where the gods had descended from the stars in their "flying boats" and turned mud and water into their new kingdom.

Akhenaten (meaning the "effective spirit of Aten") is widely known as the pharaoh who tried to force Egypt to abandon their past religions and to adopt this new belief. And how did King Akhenaten come up with the concept of star gods? He claimed that one of those celestial beings provided him with this information and further informed him that he was a descendant of Amun, one of the star gods.

Pharaoh Akhenaten ruled for a period of 17 years, and unquestionably, he was one of the most enigmatic and controversial pharaohs to have ever ruled Egypt. Interestingly enough, he was also depicted differently than any other Pharaoh before or after him. Unlike the usual muscular king with broad shoulders and small waist, Akhenaten was depicted with some feminine aspects, not only in the face but the entire body. He was portrayed with narrow shoulders, wider hips, a pot belly, a long face with clearly long slanted eyes, and most surprisingly—an elongated head. In fact, Queen Nefertiti, his wife, as well as their children, were also depicted with elongated heads. Could those be just depictions though? Not really! Surprisingly, in excavations that took place in 1907, Akhenaten's body was found, and just like in past depictions, he was found to have an oversized elongated skull! A 2010 DNA test on King Tutankhamen revealed that not only he was the son of Akhenaten, but amazingly enough, he also had an elongated skull!

Could this be another case of deformation, or some genetic transmission from father to son? Is it possible that King Akhenaten, as he claimed for himself, was a human-extraterrestrial offspring?

Impossible, some skeptics say. Such assertions can only be myths. Is it, though? From the beginning of time, our ancestors reported hybrids between humans and "gods." In fact, how do we explain the very same assertions in the Holy Bible? Even in a "modern" religion such as Christianity, we find stories of divine beings" or angels if you wish, that often enough came down to Earth to procreate with human females! How is this different? How is this even possible? Do spiritual entities have the physical need to procreate, or were these beings flesh and blood ETs that were mistaken as gods, or angels, if you wish?

> Now it came about, when men began to multiply on the face of the land, and daughters were born to them, that the sons of God saw that the daughters of men were beautiful; and they took wives for themselves, whomever they chose. [57] (Genesis, 6:1–2.)

> When the sons of God came in unto the daughters of men, and they bore children to them, the same became mighty men which were of old, men of renown. [58] (Genesis 6:4.)

Were "the sons of god" as described in the Bible truly spiritual beings, or was this a classic case of mistaken identity? Is it possible that these celestial visitors were the same flesh and blood anthropomorphic gods described by the Sumerians, the Hindus, and others? And is it possible that the reason they looked like humans, or better yet we look like them, is because we were genetically created in their image, as the Bible and the Sumerian texts best explain.

> Let *us* make man in *our* image, after *our* likeness. [59] (Genesis 1:25.)

The Sumerians, the Babylonians, the Egyptians, the Hebrew, the Chinese, the Greeks, and the Romans—as well as the Christians and Muslims—all describe and insist on similar stories in their holy scripts. There are also many similar stories of "star people" who visited Earth and mixed with humans among several smaller tribes in the American and African continents. After looking into all the different cultures and faiths, a clear pattern emerges. How can it be that every religious text of every culture, over the millennia, asserted that not only "celestial" beings created man, but occasionally they also procreated with humans as well? Is it possible that all these stories passed down from one generation to another, to be all myths and superstitions—or is it possible that there is some truth to this testimony?

In Mali, a country located in West Africa, lives a primitive tribe of people, called the Dogon.

According to anthropologists, the Dogon are thought to be of an Egyptian descent, while their religion, as well as their legends, go back as far as 3000 BC. It appears that very little has changed for these people over the past few thousand years. They still live in hut houses and perform their ceremonial dances to honor their gods, just as they did thousands of years earlier. What is fascinating about this primitive tribe, though, is not that they are of Egyptian descent, but their demonstration of incredible astronomical knowledge.

During the 1920s, when for the first time French anthropologists began documenting the Dogon stories and legends, they learned that the Dogon were already fully aware of Jupiter's 4 major moons, the rings around Saturn, the fact that the Moon is "dry and dead," and that the planets in our solar system revolved around our Sun. They claimed that this knowledge was as old as the age of their tribe. Tribal depictions and artifacts, in fact, further corroborated that this knowledge was going back at least 700 years. How is it possible for such a primitive tribe in Africa to know so much about our solar system hundreds of years before the telescope was invented?

Amazingly enough, though, their astronomical knowledge was not just limited within our solar system. The anthropologists were told about a star system, invisible to the naked eye that exists around the star Sirius. The Dogon claimed that there are two smaller stars that revolve around Sirius. One of these revolves around Sirius every 50 years and, as the Dogon claimed, this is a very heavy star as it is made of a metal that is the "heaviest material found in the universe." The second of the two stars, as they further explained, is even smaller and revolves around Sirius once every 6 years.

While the existence and trajectory of Sirius B was first discovered in 1864, it was not until 1915 when it was first accepted that Sirius B could be a white dwarf, which as the Dogon suggested, is made of a matter that is incredibly dense and extremely heavy. While Sirius B is smaller than Earth, it weighs about 8 times more than our own Sun.

The Dogon story was so incredible when it was first published that some skeptics immediately suggested that someone must have provided this information to the Dogon within 2-3 years after the discovery was made public, and just before the French anthropologists got to document their stories. Is this possible? Without the modern communication means, just after the turn of the 20th century, someone deliberately made a point to educate the Dogon of our latest astronomical discoveries? And if so, how do we explain that Dogon archaeological artifacts and certain depictions reveal that they possessed this knowledge at least since the 1300s? If so, let's not forget that during the 14th century the prevailing cosmological understanding in Europe, was that the earth was flat, had four corners, as the church often proclaimed, and it was permanently stable, in a universe where everything else revolved around it!

Unbelievably enough, this mystery and debate did not end with the discovery of Sirius B though. In 1995, two French researchers published an article in the prestigious *Journal of Astronomy and Astrophysics* labeled, "Is Sirius a Triple Star?" According to the two astronomers, Daniel Benest and J. L Duvent, Sirius C is smaller than Sirius B and revolves around Serius A every six years, just as the Dogon predicted! Is this just another incredible lucky guess from the Dogon? If not, where did this primitive tribe obtained such information?

According to the Dogon religion, roughly 5,000 years ago, an extraterrestrial race came to Earth from a planet revolving around Sirius C. These visitors called the Nommo are whom the Dogon credited with their astrological knowledge. The Dogon insist that the Nommo came to Earth in a "glowing star" that, as it descended to Earth, caused "a whirling dust storm." They also talked about "a flame that went out as the ark touched the ground".

While obviously the Nommo were worshipped as gods, the Dogon carved statues of them always depicting Nommo as humanoid beings with elongated heads, resembling those of ancient Egypt and Nazca, Peru. Is this just another bizarre coincidence? Is it possible that the "gods" or "divine beings" many of our ancestors came in contact with had elongated heads? Was this a "divine feature" and perhaps a characteristic that separated us humans from the "gods"? And let's not forget that unlike all religious illustrations of "angels," according to the Bible and early Christian testimony, these "divine" beings did not make public appearances with large wings attached on their backs. How were they recognized, then? For example, just right before the destruction of Sodom and Gomorrah, angels in human form somehow convinced Abraham of their "divinity" before their message was accepted. How did Abraham recognize these entities though? As religious scholars also tell us, what was that "divine" feature angels possessed, in order to be recognized and separated beyond a shadow of a doubt from other human beings? Was it their elongated skulls, perhaps?

In North America, the Zuni Indians inhabited an area in New Mexico for about 2,000 years. In this part of the world, etched in stone, there are what appear to be supernatural beings, star formations, and other depictions of creatures that the Zuni describe as being the "Star People."

Just like the Sumerians, the Zuni tribe believes that their creators were celestial beings that descended here from the stars in their "flying ships" and seeded the Earth.

Huang Di, meaning the "yellow emperor" in Chinese, is considered to be the first emperor of China, the father of all Chinese people and the originator of the Chinese culture. He lived and ruled in China for nearly a hundred years, around the 27th century BC. Among other things, he is credited for the unification of China and for having brought science, written language, and for traditional Chinese medicines, including acupuncture. His wife is credited with teaching people how to produce silk and make clothing.

During his life, Huang Di authored various books, and he is known as the inventor of many strange devices. One of those devices was called "the south-pointing chariot." The name of the device was attributed to a mechanical figure of a man standing on the chariot, whose outstretched arm always pointed southward. This was an ingenious navigation device that somehow worked without the need of magnets!

Another more mysterious gadget than the south-pointing chariot was a device that translates as "the tripod." According to the texts, this tripod stood between 3-4 meters (about 15 feet) in height, was filled with "hundreds of energies inside," and "a curious man could not see inside it," thus insinuating the object was solid. The mysterious tripod—or better yet, tripods, as there were many—were capable of storing "knowledge and data" and apparently recorded the life and times of Huang Di.

According to the story, a tripod always "knew" favorable and unfavorable signs and knew "that which exists and that which has disappeared". It was claimed that when these tripods functioned, they emitted voices and sounds. So what were these tripods? Were they solid objects, like three-sided pyramids? Is it possible that they were some sort of communication devices? Oddly enough, according to the story, all tripods, including the one installed by Huang Di on the summit of Lake Mountain (18 kilometers northeast of Zhaoqing) were pointed toward the stars and the Syuan Yuan constellation known today as the Leo constellation.

Although no one will ever know what these devices were or what purpose they served, is it possible though, that they were the inspiration behind the mysterious pyramids of China? Is it possible that once we are able to explore some of these pyramids, we find they contain ancient knowledge and data as the Huang Di tripods did? And if the Huang Di tripods were not the inspiration behind the megalithic pyramids just north of Xian, what else could have inspired their construction. Let it be known, some of these pyramids are taller than the step pyramids of Central America and some of the early ones in Egypt.

As bizarre and mysterious as these tripod devices were, the most fantastic and controversial part in the story of Huang Di, was his ability to fly at enormous speeds in a "flying machine" that emitted "thunder." A particular text describes that Huang Di's amazing transportation device was originated in "a land where the suns are born." Amazingly enough, this "flying dragon," as this device was called, was not portrayed as some mythical creature, but as a flying machine similar to the "fire-spitting dragons," which descended from the stars and "gods emerged out of their bellies!" According to the same story, one of Huang Di's assistants was also known as the "prince of thunder." Was this man perhaps the "navigator" of the "flying dragon"?

This, without a doubt, is an interesting story, but even more interesting is the writer's notion that the tremendous speed of the "flying dragon" had an impact on the movement of time! This is remarkable since we all know Einstein first published his special theory of relativity in 1905!

According to Einstein's theory, for a person who travels at 99% of the speed of light, time moves slower. In fact, for every year traveling at that constant speed, seven years lapse here on Earth! How is it possible, though, that such an incredible theory that involves time dilation and special relativity was alleged nearly 4,500 years ago?

After a long life (100 years to be exact), Huang Di made his preparations for his "return to the skies." According to the same legend, a flying dragon descended and took him away to the same place in the sky where his tripods were pointing.

Today, as Huang-Di's life was not thoroughly documented, as in the case of the First Dynasty that followed (1766 BC–1122 BC), mainstream Chinese scholars argue that Huang Di must have been a mythical figure, although they cannot quite explain how the complex Chinese writing system coincides with Huang Di's period.

Another incredible story that emerged out of central China nearly a half a century ago was the find of the mysterious Dropa Discs.

The discovery took place in the northeastern region of the massive Tibetan Plateau, on the remote Bayan Kara Ula Mountains, today renamed Bayan HarSha. It is an isolated area in the Qinghai Province, ranging from 2,000 to 5,000 meters in elevation and is located just north of the most eastern tip of the autonomous region of Tibet.

Details of this controversial story were first published in 1962 in the July edition of a German Magazine called *The Vegetarian Universe* and in an article called "UFOs in Pre-history?"

A few years later, in 1968, the story resurfaced in *Sputnik Magazine*, a Soviet magazine that was published in many languages from 1967–1991. It was intended to be the Soviet equivalent of the *Reader's Digest*. It was the article in this magazine that prompted the renowned author Eric Von Daniken, to investigate the story further by traveling to Russia and ultimately to include it in his book *Return to the Stars*.

The core of the story is based on a 1938 cave exploration that had taken place in the remote, most easterly region of the Kunlum mountain chain, led by a team of archaeologists with the Chinese Academy of Sciences in Beijing. In one of the many caves examined, they discovered inscriptions on the walls. Deeper into the cave, they found several tombs that contained strange-looking skeletal remains, measuring four feet in length and having unusually large skulls. Along with the skeletons, they found 716 stone discs. The discs were 30cm in diameter, 1cm thick, they had a hole in the center, like a phonogram disc, and each was engraved with strange looking hieroglyphs.

After several attempts and more than 20 years later, it was reported that the message on the discs was finally deciphered by another team with the Beijing Academy of Prehistory. According to their findings, the discs described the crash-landing of an extraterrestrial spacecraft 12,000 years ago. The following are some excerpts from the translation:

> The Dropa came out of the clouds in their airplanes…
> before sunrise, our men women and children hid in the
> caves ten times… when they finally understood the sign
> language of the Dropa, they realized the newcomers had
> peaceful intentions… [60]

Although initially the Chinese Academy of Sciences tried to ban the publication of these findings, by 1961–1962, the story eventually was published and obviously provided the basis for the article that followed in the *The Vegetarian Universe* magazine, soon after.

In the following years, skeptics continued to dismiss this "preposterous" story as a tale imagined either by Eric Von Daniken or David Aragon, but in doing so, they didn't realize that their assumption leads to a chronological paradox. As previously mentioned, Eric Von Daniken indicated in his book that he learned of this story in 1968, six or seven years after the story was first published in *Vegetarian Universe*. For those who claim that David Aragon created the story in his own book titled *Sungods in Exile*, once again they are mistaken as that book was published in 1978.

In regards to the discs, several skeptics today dismiss the significance of this discovery as they claim the Dropa discs simply resemble the "bi" discs, a known ingredient in the Chinese culture for thousands of years. What they fail to recognize though is that the bi disc tradition could very well date as far back as 10,000 years ago, thus coinciding with the same period of the Dropa Discs. If so, and since nobody seems to know for certain what inspired the bi disc tradition, is it reasonable to assume that the Dropa incident and the Dropa discs are the originators of the Chinese tradition that followed?

Today, the best interpretation we have on the bi discs is that since antiquity they were considered a "sky" symbol and they were buried with the dead, to accompany them in the afterworld, or better yet the "sky"! If this strange tradition though, is not associated with the Dropa what other incident could have taken place to help spark such custom? How, otherwise, does a disc with a hole in the center, suggest a connection with the sky, burials, or the divine? Just like the Sumerian story of the Great Flood that found its way into our holy books 6,000 years later, is it possible to assume that all bi discs over the millennia were commemorating a particular incident? We all know how important divine symbols can be to humanity. For example, for Christians, the cross is clearly one of those symbols that not only represent religious beliefs, but as we all know, it also memorializes an actual event that took place more than 2,000 years ago. So just like the Christians who faithfully continued to adhere to their symbols and traditions for thousands of years, isn't it possible that the Chinese followed in the same manner a tradition that commemorates their contact with Dropa?

Of course, there are those who entirely dismiss the story due to the recently lost evidence. Before rushing to dismiss the story though, we should not overlook the fact that the 20th century was one of the most turbulent centuries in human history. And for the Chinese this was not an exception. As we all know, China suffered tremendously under the Proletarian Cultural Revolution that took place from 1966 until 1976. During this period, many people lost their lives and innumerable cultural treasures and objects of value became the victim of looting, theft, and destruction.

Just as in other upheavals, such as the invasion of Iraq by the United States in 2003, where entire museums were cleared out by looters, or during the massive public attempt of the Egyptian people to overthrow their government—in every such case, looting, theft, and destruction always takes place.

The decade-long Cultural Revolution in China not only provides an explanation for many missing artifacts, but also provides a further insight into why the "planned displacement" of so many surviving artifacts from Beijing museums and universities to the surrounding provinces. But let's be honest, though. Even if all the evidence were still available, would the skeptics ever consider such a preposterous claim?

Such is also the criticism, which the following relic has gone through, regardless of past scientific tests performed and their recent conclusions.

# INEXPLICABLE SKULLS
# OF ANTIQUITY

*The 'Starchild' Project*
*The Andahuaylillas Skull - A Human-Extraterrestrial Hybrid*

A recent discovery of a very bizarre looking skull is currently leading some scientists into an unfamiliar territory where, once all tests are concluded, yet another accidental find, may prove to be a very significant discovery. In essence, when all tests are completed, and the results are conclusive, this skull may ultimately provide irrefutable evidence that not only were we visited by extraterrestrials in the past, but now, there is proof of a human-extraterrestrial hybrid!

First, this astonishing artifact must undergo a few more tests, and most of all must withstand the heavy skepticism that it is exposed to! The skull's ongoing study is known as the "Starchild Project".

Apparently, a young lady found the skull inside a mine tunnel in the 1930s, about 160 kilometers southwest of Chihuahua, Mexico. The unusual skull was part of a child-size skeleton that was found alongside another normal adult-size skeleton. Both remains were facing up, and they were barely covered with a few inches of dirt.

The young lady was able to collect and bring both skulls back to United States, and she kept them in her home, in El Paso, Texas. Years later, once she passed away, the skulls became the property of Mr. Ray and Melanie Young. Mrs. Young, who coincidentally was a nurse, knew right away that the anomalies on the Starchild skull, did not match with any known pathological condition. In 1999, while she still kept on thinking that the deformation could be ultimately explained by some extremely rare disease, she sought the help of Mr. Lloyd Pye, who had the means and contacts to have the Starchild skull properly tested. Indeed, under Mr. Pye the Starchild skull began to undergo a thorough examination.

The tests started right away with X-rays and radiocarbon dating. The first radiocarbon dating was done in 1999 by the University of California at Riverside, and the second test in 2004 at Beta Analytic in Miami. Both tests produced the same results and estimated that the skull is 900 years old.

For more than 10 years, the skull became the subject of a thorough examination, including extraction of DNA. While a regular DNA test in 2003 was deemed unsuccessful, in the early part of 2010, an American team of geneticists began a new series of tests, with an attempt to recover the Starchild's nuclear DNA while using a brand-new method called the shotgun recovery technique. The analysis was a success. Out of 3 billion base pairs in the skull's genome, several thousand were recovered. Amazingly enough though, the nuclear DNA fragments that were repeatedly analyzed by the National Institute of Health BLAST (Basic Local Alignment Search Tool) program indicated that a substantial percentage of the Starchild's DNA has "no significant similarity" to any other known DNA on earth!

For those less familiar, the United States National Institute of Health contains the largest DNA database found anywhere on the planet while the BLAST program, is one of the most widely used bioinformatic programs, which allows researchers to compare a query sequence with a library or database of sequences.

Once the testing was completed, the BLAST report indicated that 265 base pairs from its nuclear DNA perfectly matched a gene on human chromosome 1. This conclusion indicates that part of the nuclear DNA of the Starchild is from a human mother. Surprisingly enough though, the same report indicated that a string of base pairs, 342 nucleotides long, had no matching reference when those were compared to the institution's databank! This declaration is extremely important because, in other words, they are saying those belong to a nonrecognizable life form!

Of course, other than this anomaly, several more abnormal characteristics in the skull's physiology raise additional questions. For starters, the skull, unlike a typical human, is wider on the top (more like a heart shape) and it leads to a smaller, very narrow chin. It is estimated that the overall cavity of the skull would hold approximately 200cubic centimeters more brain than a normal skull. Its cranium bone is half as thick, in comparison to a normal human. More strangely, a lab analysis indicated that the Starchild skull contains very high properties of carbon and calcium, while its oxygen and phosphorus contents are the lowest. This, in itself, defies logical explanation. A regular human bone contains nearly the opposite levels. It is very high in calcium and phosphorus, while its oxygen, and especially its carbon levels, are the lowest. This major difference in biochemistry makes the Starchild skull be more like tooth enamel rather than a bone as we know it.

When a small piece of the skull was cut out for DNA analysis, it was discovered that it contained some strange-looking fibers that were embedded into the bone. As the tool used to cut out the skull was not able to cut cleanly through these fibers, it was determined that these fibers were providing this skull additional reinforcement. Furthermore, unlike a normal skull that ultimately over time turns to pure white, the Starchild skull retained some of its color, including some red substance that appeared to be heavier around the bone marrow cavities. And this is not all! When comparing it to a typical human skull, there are many more significant differences.

It was further determined that the Starchild skull lacks frontal sinuses. Its ears appear to be slightly lower than usual and a little forward. Also, judging by its design, it was determined that it had much smaller chewing muscles, as well as a much smaller and narrower lower jaw. Finally, its eye sockets are much shallower and appear to be in an upright angle position, rather than the normal horizontal position. By the way, a normal human eye socket is about five centimeters deep and "cones" straight backward. The Starchild's eye sockets are only about 2.25 centimeters deep while its optic nerves and foramens appear to be pointing low and toward the center of the face, near the nose. The base of the skull further indicated that it had a very narrow neck, possibly half as wide as a normal person. Finally, while an X-ray early on revealed that the skull had teeth waiting to come down, leading scientists earlier to believe the Starchild was that of a child, another test in 2010, which included an actual tooth extraction, revealed that the Starchild was actually an adult at the time of death!

Another incredible discovery that attracted attention around the globe and caused a widespread speculation as to what could it be, are the mummified remains of an anthropomorphic being with an elongated head found near Cusco, Peru, in 2011. The unusual skeleton was discovered by Renato Davila Riquelme, a museum curator, in the hills of his hometown of Andahuaylillas. The remains were that of child-size skeleton with a large elongated skull, triangular in shape measuring about 20 inches (50cm), and a body measuring about the same size. Only a single arm remains attached to the body. The second arm—as well as both legs—were never found.

According to Renato Davila Riquelme, soon after its discovery, one Russian and two Spanish anthropologists who examined the controversial find, tentatively declared that the skull is not that of a human being. These claims caught the attention of Dr. Theo Paredes, a renowned local anthropologist who offered to examine the skull further. As he could not conclusively identify either whether the specimen was human or not, he convinced Riquelme to submit the remains for clinical tests and authentication by medical experts.

The initial examination conducted by Dr. Alcides Vargas, Clinic Director of Clinica Pardo, corroborated the authenticity of the remains. In addition to the skull's unusual size, Dr. Vargas also pointed out that this person had very large protruding eyes, much larger than anything normally seen in human beings, and unusually small nasal cavity. He also noticed that the "fontanelle" spot on top of the cranium was still open, a common characteristic among infants and children up to two years of age. Strangely though, while the soft spot on the cranium indicated that the remains could have been that of a child, full grown molars proved otherwise. This person clearly was an adult at the time of death.

A closer examination by Dr. Erick Flores, including an X-ray, revealed that the skull did not belong to a victim with hydrocephalus disease. In fact, other than its unusual size and odd deformities, tests indicated that the large skull had no known disorders. For those not familiar, hydrocephalus is a developmental disability in which the victim's brain cavity fills with spinal fluid, causing the head to swell like a balloon. If it goes untreated and the fluid is not drained from the skull, hydrocephalus disease is fatal.

To answer certain concerns regarding whether the skull was subjected to intentional cranial deformation, a known practice among the Nazca people during that time, Dr. Elisa Orellana, conducted additional tests which included a CT scan. After a thorough examination, she concluded that the skull was not deliberately forced in any way. Furthermore, Dr. Carlos Perez, a neurologist who also conducted a series of tests, also concluded that other than its inexplicable proportions, the skull was "normal" otherwise. Dr. Perez who also calculated the volume of the skull, determined that it was 50% larger than that of a typical person.

Additional testing established the radiocarbon age of the skull to be around 700 years old, thus ruling out the possibility that the remains could belong to an unknown subhuman species from our distant past. Finally, while mitochondrial DNA testing identified its mother as a human, further analysis could not specify what species could have fathered this being.

So, what can this be? Is it possible that these are the remains of a human-extraterrestrial hybrid as some of the experts cautiously suggested? If so, this certainly corresponds to past Incan myths and religion which talk about an anthropomorphic being with an elongated head, large eyes and a flattened nose. Is it possible that these legends were not legends after all? Most importantly, was this anthropomorphic creature and others that looked like it, the inspiration behind the practice of skull deformation among the Nazca people nearby?

# MYSTERIOUS PLACES

*Prehistoric Human Settlements in South Africa
and the Middle East --- Gobekli Tepe*

Not too long ago, mainstream science made the announcement that geneticists, through DNA analysis, concluded that all humans trace back to an original pair of humans—an Adam and Eve if you will, or to a small group of individuals that originated in South Africa roughly 200,000 years ago. From there, they ultimately migrated around the planet.

Setting a thousand questions aside about this announcement, like what possibly could have triggered the sudden mutation 200,000 years ago, or what particular conditions in South Africa could have contributed to this transformation; do we have any physical evidence otherwise that could support a huge population of *Homo sapiens* in South Africa so long ago? Actually, it seems that we do! Interestingly enough, the recent scientific Adam and Eve revelation coincided with yet another incredible discovery in the region of South Africa. It was the finding of prehistoric gold mines.

Although without a doubt, both announcements were of great significance; unfortunately, when comparing them to established historical accounts, the two stories—or better yet two realities—contradict one another. How is it possible that early humans were somehow preprogrammed, not only with a primal need to survive but also with tremendous hunger for gold? This is a great paradox, unless of course the Sumerians were right all along, and humans were purposely placed in the land of Abzu by their creators with instructions to mine this gold for the gods. Was this Sumerian claim just a bizarre coincidence? If so, how do we explain that the Zulu, a large South African tribe, in their own testimony further corroborate the Sumerian claims?

As the Sumerians asserted, Zulu legends speak of a time when celestial visitors came to Earth to excavate for gold and other resources! Is this just a striking coincidence, another fantastic story from a primitive tribe, or is it time perhaps to pay closer attention to some of these legends?

If a large group of people, however, were involved in gold mining, where are the signs to indicate their presence in the area? Clearly, such an organized activity could not have taken place without the proper housing for those involved. Surprisingly though, another somewhat accidental discovery in this region, if proven to be old enough, can very well be the prehistoric settlement that housed the thousands of primitive workers involved in the ancient gold mines. Actually, the ruins on this site are just an outline of foundation walls of the structures that once stood there. And just like the Nazca site, these low-to-the-ground ruins are best visible from a higher altitude.

The huge site that easily covers an area of more than 1,000 square miles is covered with thousands of ruins of various circular structures that are grouped in small clusters like beehives. Often, it appears that each "beehive group" is also enclosed by another circular perimeter wall.

Judging by their looks, it seems that each cluster—or small "compound" if you will—could have been occupied by a small group of people. The smaller circles within and/or around the larger compound enclosures could be those of round huts with thatch roofs that provided the primary housing, while the larger enclosures were to contain animals and/or denote personal space within the group. The outer wall of each "beehive" structure was there for added security. Interestingly, and just as in modern cities, many of these small compounds that most likely housed different family groups are bunched together. Also, under closer observation, it becomes evident that few of these individual structures are united by an enclosed path—a suggestion that their residents decided to join their "households" at one point or another.

A huge concentration of these primitive assemblies can be found just eastward of the city of Machadodorp. They run from north to south, between Machadodorp and Emqwenya, and they get really dense as they cross over route R541. From there, they continue to scatter southward for several miles on both sides of route R36.

Another small scarce concentration of these structures is also located just west of Mkhazeni. This find points to a second, smaller, and completely separate settlement from the one near Machadodorp.

Although, at first glance, it is easy to confuse these ancient structures with just about anything including animal corrals, under a closer examination, they actually resemble the ruins of a 10,000 year-old site found on the island of Cyprus in the eastern Mediterranean.

At an official archaeological site called Khirokitia, due to a village nearby carrying the same name, one can observe a similar type of round "beehive" structures. Although they may not be as old, large, and vast as the African site, the tiny Cyprus settlement dates back to 8000 BC. Just like each cluster of ruins in Africa, it was also encircled with an outer wall for extra protection.

*Khirokitia ruins, 8000BC.*

*Khirokitia ruins (8000BC) reconstructed.*

Another well known site that features circular structures enclosed within a perimeter wall is the ancient city of Tell es-Sultan in Palestine, otherwise known as Jericho. Archaeological excavations there showed that the oldest structures in Jericho date back to the Natufian period, between 10th and 8th millennia BC.

Ancient foundations of circular structures resembling those of South Africa were also recently found in Syria, Jordan, and Saudi Arabia. As the structures in Cyprus and Palestine though, seem to be far more refined and preserved than those in Africa, Syria and Jordan, this leads to the conclusion that the latter may be much older settlements. So, while without a doubt, all these prehistoric sites worth further attention, another location yet with circular structures was recently uncovered in Turkey.

On February 19, 2010, *Newsweek* published an article, entitled "History in the Remaking: A Temple Complex in Turkey that Predates Even the Pyramids Is Rewriting the Human Evolution."

The site of Gobekli Tepe is located in southeastern Turkey, roughly 30 kilometers from Syria. As the title of the article claims, this is a place where archeologists literally stumbled on one of the most incredible archaeological finds in recent history. They began to uncover a vast complex that is so old it pre-dates the Great Pyramid by at least 7,000 years.

The huge ceremonial site features massive terrazzo floor circles, surrounded by huge carved pillars that call to mind the monoliths at Easter Island. The biggest circular structure uncovered so far is about 27 meters across (about 95 feet), while the tallest pillars that make the structure are more than 5 meters (about 17 feet) tall. This massive temple complex is believed to have been built immediately after the last ice age and about 12,000 or 13,000 years ago! Although most of the T-shaped, 10-ton stone pillars have carvings of animals on them, many of the biggest ones are carved as humanoids with arms, shoulders, elbows, and jointed fingers—and they appear to be towering humanlike deities.

According to Klaus Schmidt this site covers an area of about 22 acres and is so much material to excavate here that archaeologists could dig for the next 50 years and barely scratch the surface! So what was taking place here? Moreover, how is it possible that primitive "hunters and gatherers" were ever able to organize and undertake such a project, if according to mainstream academia, the people of this region did not have the knowledge, the technology, or the governing institutions 13,000 years ago in order to undertake such a project. Where did the desire or technological know-how come from in order for these people to be able to carve, move, and erect the 40-60 ton T-shape pillars that characterize the entire site? And let's not forget that these mega structures pre-date Stonehenge by 6,000 years! Is it possible that such a monumental task was undertaken by a mob of primitive hunters and gathers on a part-time basis? Most likely, not! Finally, should we assume that there is a connection between the huge round structures at Gobekli Tepe and the ruins of Khirokitia in Cyprus, or those found in southeast Africa and Middle East?

Although no one knows for certain, the evidence that support an advanced civilization in the Mediterranean during our prehistory are overwhelming.

# EPILOGUE

It is no secret that only few stories have the power to captivate people's imagination more than those that remain unresolved. Accounts of past lost civilizations, strange aerial phenomena, unexplained encounters and cryptic codes, unquestionably continue to tease our minds with their intrigue.

Inadvertently, our history is full of such real life riddles that neither scientists or researchers can quite explain. And while many of these puzzles, which often are passed down from one generation to another, sound so incredible that they appear to be stories of pure fiction, from time to time, and more often than we realize, they turn out to be true.

Indeed, a claim like "humanity traces back to a primary couple" or a small group of individuals, at one point may have sounded like a fantasy. Not anymore! Today, more than ever before, as science is beginning to confirm that most ancient claims are real, and what once was considered to be science fiction is turning into a science fact, isn't it time perhaps to pay closer attention to our ancestors stories, no matter how fantastic they may sound?

Is it true that humans were way too primitive 12,000 years ago, or as our ancestors claim, humanity advanced thousands of years earlier than anthropologists previously had realized? Ancient claims and legends of prehistoric advanced civilizations were not only reported by Plato alone, but by other cultures in the Middle east as well as in Asia.

Whether or not the submerged city off the coast of India was the lost city of Dwarka, or the prehistoric island of the Cyclades Plateau was once called Atlantis, unquestionably, these discoveries and like that of Gobekli Tepe, prove that mankind flourished much earlier in time.

If so, then it is conceivable that the eastern Mediterranean gene, haplogroup X, could have navigated to North America via island hopping and just as Plato claimed. If not, how do we otherwise explain the genetic maps which seem to corroborate Plato's account? Consequently, if the "prehistoric" Atlantians managed to sail to North America 10,000 years ago, is it so hard to accept, as the evidence also shows, that another Mediterranean civilization, like that of the Minoans, reached America during the Bronze Age? If not, who else 3,500 years ago could have regularly extracted copper from the region around the Great Lakes, and in the process, supplied the Mediterranean and especially the Egyptians with plants and spices indigenous to the New World? And, what about the Caucasian sightings reported by native Americans, including the Mayan Indians? Who were these Caucasian perpetrators that the Mayan ultimately attributed their civilization to, and furthermore, how do we otherwise explain that the Mayan architecture appears to be a hybrid of a Minoan and Mesopotamian structures?

Was the sudden rise of the oceans around 8000 BC, the event we all recognize today as the Great Flood and the catastrophe that erased our early history?

Is it possible that early humans could have evolved naturally from their primitive stage to a modern man, or is there another explanation behind the missing link in human evolution, as those who managed to unravel the human DNA maintain. More explicitly, should we discard the fact that from the beginning of time, every religion on Earth claims that humans were manipulated into existence by a "higher" power. And if so, are we absolutely certain of a spiritual power performing physical acts, or there is something more behind these claims? Is it possible, as our ancestors allege, humans are the genetic creation of the anthropomorphic gods of antiquity, who formed mankind in their own image by combining their DNA (or blood in lack of better words) with a creature from Earth (Earth as in planet) and not earth as in soil, as the Holy Bible asserts. When keeping in mind that the Old Testament of the Bible borrowed many of its stories from the much older Sumerian original, isn't it possible that when this particular story was copied, the Hebrew translators failed to differentiate the two ingredients, earth and Earth.

Consequently, can this alleged genetic creation be the answer behind the missing link in the human evolution? Have we truly evolved naturally in South Africa, or were we placed there by our creators for a particular task? And did the gods of antiquity often procreate with humans, as our religious books and ancestors proclaim? Accordingly, what could then be the origin and real identity of many modern religions? As the Old Testament of the Bible seems to be a copy of an older Sumerian original, is it possible then that the Hebrew, Christians, and Muslims—as they all share the same stories and religious content—all unknowingly still worship, at least partially, the same Sumerian stories and beliefs from 6,000 years ago? How significant is that?

In conclusion, what happened to our implied creators? Who were these otherworldly beings? Did they truly have elongated heads, and did they come to Earth from another planet as our ancestors claim? Most importantly, did they leave Earth a long time ago; or since in the last few centuries mankind exploded out of control—to avoid confrontation—they morphed themselves into the all familiar UFO sightings and continued their earthly endeavors, while giving us time to further evolve before their next coming?

"If you have only one piece of circumstantial evidence, carrying that evidence to a specific conclusion is prone to significant error. However, when you have numerous pieces of circumstantial evidence all pointing in the same direction, carrying them, collectively, to a specific conclusion is usually quite reliable."

Conclusions Drawn from
Circumstantial Evidence

# ABOUT ATLANTIS

Atlantis (in Greek, Ἀτλαντὶς νῆσος, "island of Atlas") is a legendary island first mentioned in Plato's dialogues Timaeus and Critias, written about 360 BC. According to Plato, Atlantis was a naval power that approximately 9600 BC had conquered many parts of Europe and Africa (Wikipedia, the Free Encyclopedia).

"For it is related in our records how once upon a time your State stayed the course of a mighty host, which, starting from a distant point in the Atlantic ocean, was insolently advancing to attack the whole of Europe, and Asia to boot. For the ocean there was at that time navigable; for in front of the mouth which you Greeks call, as you say, 'the pillars of Heracles,' there lay an island which was larger than Libya and Asia together; and it was possible for the travelers of that time to cross from it to the other islands, and from the islands to the whole of the continent over against them which encompasses that veritable ocean. For all that we have here, lying within the mouth of which we speak, is evidently a haven having a narrow entrance; but that yonder is a real ocean, and the land surrounding it may most rightly be called, in the fullest and truest sense, a continent" - (Timaeus 24e–25a, R. G. Bury translation [Loeb Classical Library]).

"An island comprising mostly mountains in the northern portions and along the shore, and encompassing a great plain of an oblong shape in the south "extending in one direction three thousand stadia [about 555 km; 345 mi], but across the center inland it was two thousand stadia [about 370 km; 230 mi]." Fifty stadia [9 km; 6 mi] from the coast was a mountain that was low on all sides... broke it off all round about... the central island itself was five stades in diameter [about 0.92 km; 0.57 mi]" - (Critias 113, 116a, Bury translation).

"But at a later time there occurred portentous earthquakes and floods, and one grievous day and night befell them, when the whole body of your warriors was swallowed up by the earth, and the island of Atlantis in like manner was swallowed up by the sea and vanished; wherefore also the ocean at that spot has now become impassable and unsearchable, being blocked up by the shoal mud which the island created as it settled down" - (Timaeus 25c–d, Bury translation).

"The consequence is, that in comparison of what then was, there are remaining in small islets only the bones of the wasted body, as they may be called, all the richer and softer parts of the soil having fallen away, and the mere skeleton of the country being left. But in former days, and in the primitive state of the country, what are now mountains were regarded as hills; and the plains are they are now termed, of Phelleus were full of rich earth, and there was abundance of wood in the mountains. Of this last the traces still remain, for there are some of the mountains which now only afford sustenance to bees, whereas not long ago there were still remaining roofs cut from the trees growing there, which were of a size sufficient to cover the largest houses; and there were many other high trees, bearing fruit, and abundance of food for cattle" - (*The Dialogues of Plato: Republic*/Timaeus. Critias–Plato, Benjamin Jowett).

# NOTES

[1] "Antikythera Mechanism," Wikipedia, the Free Encyclopedia, http://en.wikipedia.org/wiki/antikythera_mechanism.

[2] "Atlantis," Wikipedia, the Free Encyclopedia, http://en.wikipedia.org/wiki/Atlantis.

[3] Ibid.

[4] James C. Chatters, "Kennewick Man," http://oneyahweh.com/w/archives/201.

[5] Charles Gallenkamp, "Maya: The Riddle and Rediscovery of a Lost Civilization," 57.

[6] T. J. O'Brien, "Fair Gods and Feathered Serpents."

[7] John D. Baldwin, "The Phoenician Theory," Wikipedia, the Free Encyclopedia, http://en.Wikipedia.org/wiki/theory_of_phoenician_discovery_of_the_americas.

[8] Ian Driscoll and Matthew Kurtz, "Atlantis: Egyptian Genesis," 60.

[9] "Atlantis," Wikipedia, the Free Encyclopedia, http://en.wikipedia.org/wiki/atlantis#cite_ref-7.

[10] Ibid.

[11] Ibid.

[13] "Dialogues of Plato, Volume 2, Plato's Critias," Wikipedia, the Free Encyclopedia,http://en.wikipedia.org/wiki/Ancient_Greek_flood_myths#cite_ref-1.

[14] Ibid.

[15] K. Gaki-Papanastasiou, "Coastal and Marine Geospatial Technologies," 302.

[16] "Fred Hoyle," Wikipedia, the Free Encyclopedia, http://en.wikipedia.org/wiki/junkyard_tornado.

[17] "The Holy Bible, Genesis 2:11-12," http://bibleapps.com/genesis/2-12.htmwiki/havilah.

[18] Ibid., 11-14.

[19] "The Holy Bible, Genesis 2:12," http://www.biblestudytools.com/tmba/genesis/passage.aspx?q=genesis+2:11-21.

[20] "The Holy Bible, Exodus 35:5," http://www.kingjamesbibleonline.org/exodus-35-5/.

[21] "The Holy Bible, Exodus 31:52," http://www.kingjamesbibleonline.org/Numbers-31-52/.

[22] "The Holy Bible, Exodus 35:22," http://www.kingjamesbibleonline.org/Exodus-35-22/.

[23] "The Holy Bible, Haggai 2:8," http://biblehub.com/haggai/2-8.htm.

[24] "The Holy Bible, Genesis 1:26," http://www.kingjamesbibleonline.org/Genesis-1-26/.

[25] "The Holy Bible, Genesis 3:22," http://www.bibleshark.com/bible/nasb/genesis/3/.

[26] "The Holy Bible, Genesis 2:15," http://www.kingjamesbibleonline.org/Genesis-2-15/.

[27] "Enuma Elish," Wikipedia, the Free Encyclopedia, http://en.wikipedia.org/wiki/Enki.

[28] Ibid.

[29] "The Holy Bible, Corinthians 11:23-26," http://www.biblegateway.com/passage/?search=1+Corinthians+11%3A23-29&version=NIV;AMP.

[30] "Enmerkar and the Lord of Aratta," *The Electronic Text Corpus of Sumerian Literature*, http:// etcsl.orinst.ox.ac.uk/section1/tr1823. htm.

[31] Aubrey de Sélincourt, "Transcription: Tower of Babel Sources, Herodotus," *Histories*, 1.181-2, http://freeflowanimation.blog-spot.com/2012/02/transcription-tower-of-babel-sources.html.

[32] Eric N. Davis, *House of faith House of Cards.*

[33] "Ancient Flying Machines," http://atlantisonline.smfforfree2. com/index.php?topic=1659.15;wap2.

[34] "Samarangana Sutradhara," http://www.atlantisquest.com/Samar. html.

[35] James Hartman, "Flying Aircraft and Nuclear War and Other Strange Occurences of the Past, http://www.sacred-texts.com/ ufo/ourpast.htm.

[36] Mohan Gangul, "The Mahabharata of Krishna-Dwaipayana Vyasa," http://www.sacred-texts.com/hin/m16/m16001.htm.

[37] "The Holy Bible," Ezekiel 1:4-5, http://bibleapps.com/eze-kiel/1-4.htm.

[38] "The Holy Bible," Ezekiel 1:16, http://www.kingjamesbibleon-line.org/Ezekiel-1-16/.

[39] "The Holy Bible," Ezekiel 1:18, http://www.kingjamesbibleon-line.org/Ezekiel-1-18/.

[40] Ibid.

[41] "The Holy Bible," Ezekiel 1:7, http://www.kingjamesbibleonline. org/1611_Ezekiel-1-7/.

[42] "The Holy Bible," Ezekiel 1:5, http://www.kingjamesbibleonline. org/Ezekiel-1-5/.

[43] "The Holy Bible," Ezekiel 1:21, http://ebible.org/web/Ezekiel.htm.

[44] "The Holy Bible," Ezekiel 1:22-27, http://www.kingjamesbi-bleonline.org/Ezekiel-1-22/http://www.biblestudytools.com/eze-kiel/1-27-compare.html.

[45] "The Holy Bible," Ezekiel 1:9, http://www.esvbible.org/Ezekiel+1/.

[46] "The Holy Bible," Ezekiel 1:20, http://www.esvbible.org/Ezekiel+1/.

[47] "The Holy Bible," Ezekiel 1:27, http://www.esvbible.org/Ezekiel+1/.

[48] "The Holy Bible," Genesis 5:24, http://www.biblestudytools.com/genesis/5-24-compare.html.

[49] "The Holy Bible," 2 Kings 2:1-13, http://bibleapps.com/2_kings/2-11.htm.

[50] Sylvia Brown, *Secrets and Mysteries of the World.*

[51] "The Drake Equation," Wikipedia, the Free Encyclopedia, http://en.wikipedia.org/wiki/Drake_equation.

[52] "Thomas F. Mantell," Wikipedia, the Free Encyclopedia, http://en.wikipedia.org/wiki/Mantell_UFO_incident.

[53] "Japan Air Lines Flight 1628 Incident," Wikipedia, the Free Encyclopedia, http://en.wikipedia.org/wiki/Japan_Air_Lines_flight_1628_incident.

[54] "The Phoenix Lights," Wikipedia, the Free Encyclopedia, http://en.wikipedia.org/wiki/Phoenix_Lights.

[55] "Lt. Colonel Charles I. Halt Affidavit," Wikipedia, the Free Encyclopedia, http://en.wikipedia.org/wiki/Rendlesham_Forest_incident.

[56] "The Rendlesham Forest Incident," Wikipedia, the Free Encyclopedia, http://en.wikipedia.org/wiki/Rendlesham_Forest_incident.

[57] "The Holy Bible," Genesis 6:1-2, http://www.kingjamesbibleonline.org/Genesis-6-2/.

[58] "The Holy Bible," Genesis 6:4, Wikipedia, the Free Encyclopedia, http://en.wikipedia.org/wiki/Nephilim.

[59] "The Holy Bible," Genesis 1:25, http://www.biblestudytools.com/genesis/1-26-compare.html.

[60] Philip Coppens, "The Dropa Tribe and Their Stone Discs Revisited," http://www.philipcoppens.com/baian_kara_ula_upd.html.

# BIBLIOGRAPHY

"2006 O'Hare International Airport UFO Sighting." http://en.wikipedia.org/wiki/2006_O'Hare_International_airport_ufo_sighting/.

"Archaeologist 'Strikes Gold' With Finds of Ancient Nazca Iron Ore Mine in Peru." *Science Daily* (2008). http://www.sciencedaily.com/releases/2008/01/080129125405.htm.

"Atlantis." http://en.wikipedia.org/wiki/Atlantis.

"Bat Creek Inscription." http://en.wikipedia.org/wiki/Bat_Creek_Inscricption.

Belew, Bill. "NASA Confirms 'Alien' Life is Found on Earth." http://www.examiner.com/article/nasa-confirms-alien-life-is-found-on-earth.

Benest, D. and J. L. Duvent. "Is Sirius a Triple Star?" *Astronomy and Astrophysics*, (1995): 621-628. http://adsabs.harvard.edu/full/1995a&a..299..621b.

"Black Sea Deluge Hypothesis." http://en.wikipedia.org/wiki/black_sea_deluge_hypothesis.

Britt, Robert Roy. "24 Hours of Chaos: The Day the Moon Was Made." http://www.space.com

Childress, David Hatcher. "The Anti-Gravity Handbook." http://world-mysteries.com.

Connor, Steve. "DNA Tests Trace Adam to Africa." *Sunday Times.* November 9, 1997.

"Copper Mining in Michigan." http://en.wikipedia.org/wiki/copper_mining_in_michigan.Curry, Andrew. "Gobekli Tepe: The World's First Temple." (November, 2008). http://www.smithsonianmag.com/history-archaeology/gobekli-tepe.html.

"Die Glocke (The Bell)." http://en.wikipedia.org/die_glocke.

Doughton, Sandi. "Kennewick Man Yields More Secrets."http://seattletimes.com/html/localnews/2002825565_kennewick24m.html.

Doumenge, Francois. Presentation on The Mediterranean Crisis. United Nations University Headquarters. July 15, 1996.

"Elohim." http://en.wikipedia.org/wiki/Elohim.

"Enki." http://en.wikipedia.org/wiki/enki.

Ezekiel 1. *Hebrew-English Bible.* http://www.mechon-mamre.org/p/pt/pt1201.htm.

Ezekiel 1-2; Hebrews 11:1-19 (New International Version). *BibleGateway.com.* http://www.biblegateway.com/passage/?search=Ezekiel+1-2%2CHebrews+11%3A1-19&version=NIV.

"Five Baffling Discoveries That Prove Histroy Books Are Wrong." *Huff Post* (June 12, 2013).

"Flood Myth." http://en.wikipedia.org/wiki/flood_myth.

"Fred Hoyle." http://en.wikipedia.org/wiki/Fred_Hoyle.

Geoarcheology of the Cyclades During the Holocene; Does the Underwater Morphology Provide Clues for the Lost Atlantis? Coastal and Marine Geospatial Technologies, 302, K. Gaki-Papanastasiou, Edited by Dr.D.R.Green.

Genet, Am J. Hum. "DNA Haplogroup X: An Ancient Link Between Europe, Western Asia, and North America." *The American Journal of Human Genetics* (December, 1998). http://www.cell.com/AJHG/retrieve/pii/50002929707616292.

"Great Flood." *New World Encyclopedia.*

"Hall of Records." http://en.wikipedia.org/wiki/hall_of_records.

Handwerk, Brian. "Many 'Earths' Are Out There, Study Says." *National Geographic News*. April 6, 2005.

"Isle Royale." http://en.wikipedia.org/wiki/Isle_Royale.

Janku, Lumir G. "Ancient Flying Machines." http://www.world-mysteries.com/sar_7.htm.

"Japan Air Lines Flight 1628 Incident." http://en.wikipedia.org/wiki/japan_air_lines_flight_1628_incident/.

Jowett, Benjamin. *The Dialogues of Plato: Republi, Timaeus, Critias*. "Kennewick Man." http://www.en.wikipedia.org/wiki/Kennewick_man.

"Khirokitia." http://en.wikipedia.org/wiki/khirokitia.

Kiger, Patrick. "Top 10 Mass Sightings of UFOs." *National Geographic Channel*. http.//channel.nationalgeographic.com/channel/chasing-ufos/articles/top-10-masssightings-of-ufos/.

"Kukulkan." http://en.wikipedia.org/wiki/kukulkan.

Licking, Ellen. "Don't Blame the Horse: Earthquakes Toppled Ancient Cities, Stanford Geophysicist Says." (November 11, 1997). http://news.stanford.edu/pr97/971112nur.html.

"List of Reported UFO Sightings." http://en.wikipedia.org/wiki/list_of_reported_ufo_sightings.

"Mantell UFO Incident." http://en.wikipedia.org/wiki/mantel_ufo_incident.

"Maya Civilization." http://en.wikipedia.org/wiki/maya_civilization.

"Mitochondrial Eve Research: Humanity Was Genetically Divided for 100,000 Years." http://www.sciencedaily.com/releases/2008/05/080515154635.htm.

"Nazca Lines." http://en.wikipedia.org/Nazca_lines.

"Nazca Lines." *Sacred Destinations*. http://www.sacred-destinations.com/peru/nazca-lines.

"Nazi UFOs." http://en.wikipedia.org/nazi_ufos.

"Persian Gulf Once Dry, Green, and Inhabited by Humans: Implications." Biot #422: May 15, 2007.

"Phoenix Lights." http://en.wikipedia.org/wiki/phoenix_lights.

"Planets Beyond Neptune." https://en.wikipedia.org/wiki/planets_beyond_neptune.

"Plimpton 322 Tablet." http://en.wikipedia.org/wiki/Plimpton_322.

"Pliny the Elder." http://en.wikipedia.org/wiki/pliny_the_elder.

"Pre-Columbian Trans-Oceanic Contact." http://en.wikipedia.org/wiki/pre-columbian_trans-oceanic_contact.

Pye, Lloyd. "Alien Life: The Starchild Skull." http://www.lloydpye.com/intervention/alienlife-starchildskull.htm.

"Quetzalcoatl." http://en.wikipedia.org/wiki/Quetzalcoatl.

"Rendlesham Forest Incident." http://en.wikipedia.org/wiki/rendlesham_forest_incident.

Ryan, W. B., and W. C. Pitman. "Black Sea Deluge Theory." *Chemistry Daily.* http://www.chemistrydaily.com/chemisty/black_sea_deluge_theory.

Sitchin, Zacharia. *The 12th Planet.*

"Sumerians, Aliens, and Voyager 2." http://www.ufodigest.com/sumerians.html.

Symmes, Patrick. "History in the Remaking." *Newsweek.* http://www.questia.com/library/1g1-219477534/history-in-the-remaking.

"Theory of Phoenician Discovery of the Americas." http://en.wikipedia.org/wiki/Theory_of_Phoenician_Discovery_of_the_Americas.

"Timeline of Discovery of Solar System Planets and Their Moons." http://www.wikipedia.com.

Lightning Source UK Ltd.
Milton Keynes UK
UKHW011529220621
385967UK00001B/176